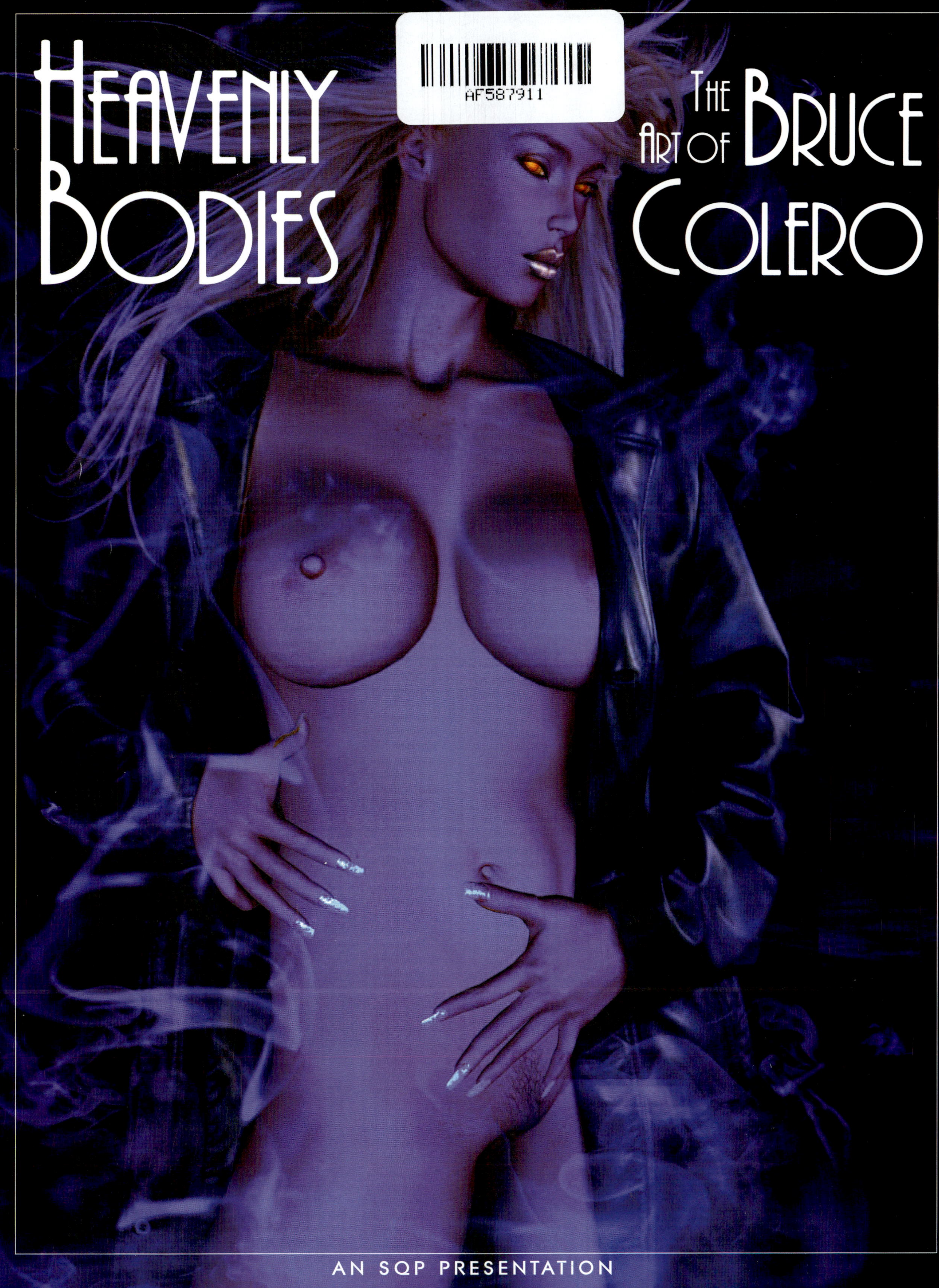

Heavenly Bodies

The Art of Bruce Colero

An SQP Presentation

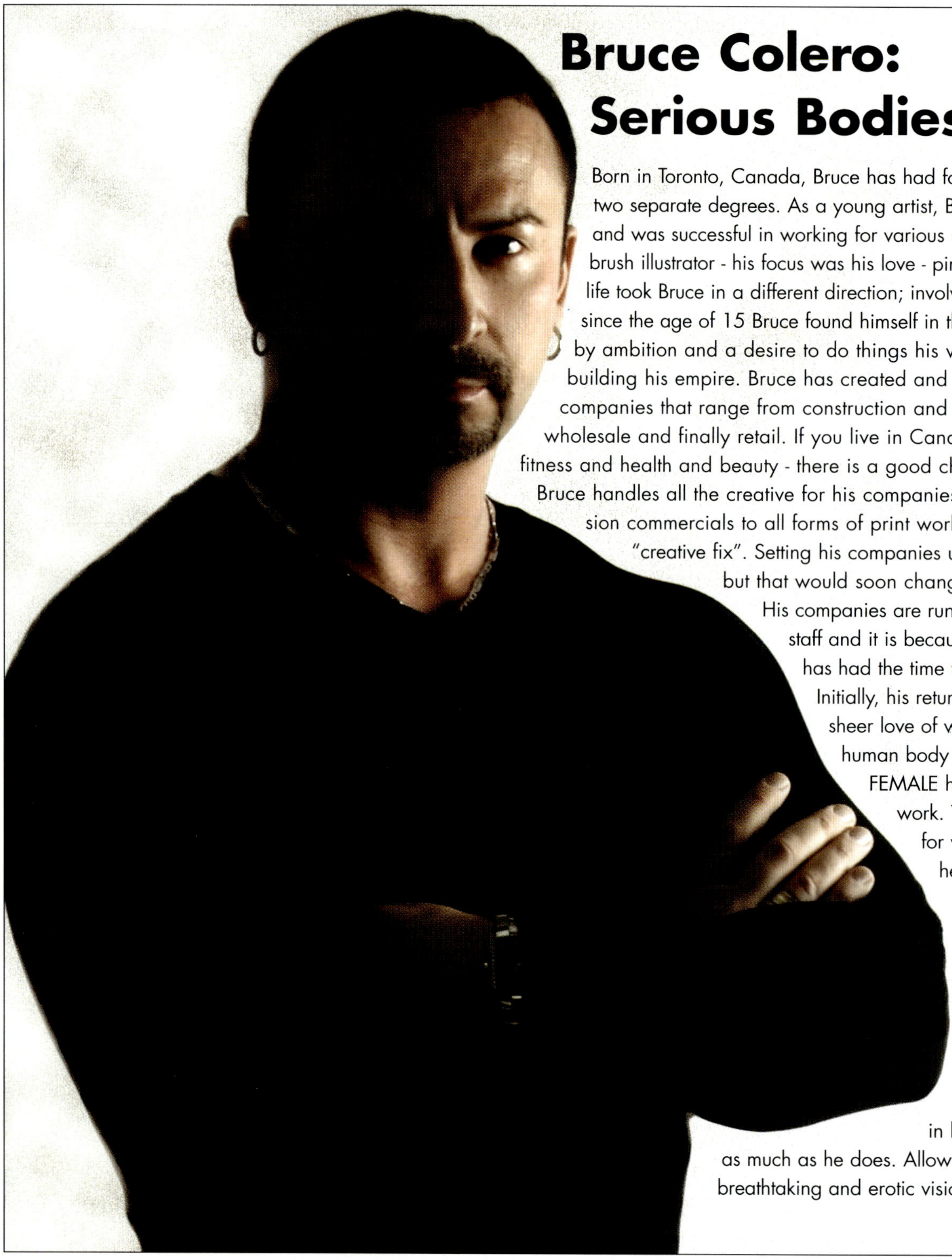

Bruce Colero: Serious Bodies of Work

Born in Toronto, Canada, Bruce has had formal instruction in fine art and holds two separate degrees. As a young artist, Bruce pursued a career in illustration and was successful in working for various magazines and agencies as an air-brush illustrator - his focus was his love - pinup and fantasy work. Years later, life took Bruce in a different direction; involved in martial arts and bodybuilding since the age of 15 Bruce found himself in the health and fitness industry. Driven by ambition and a desire to do things his way, the next 7 years were spent building his empire. Bruce has created and owns a linked infrastructure of companies that range from construction and manufacturing to distribution and wholesale and finally retail. If you live in Canada and have anything to do with fitness and health and beauty - there is a good chance Bruce Colero is a part of it. Bruce handles all the creative for his companies, ranging from radio and television commercials to all forms of print work - a satisfying way of getting his "creative fix". Setting his companies up allowed little time for painting... but that would soon change.

His companies are run by a loyal and highly competent staff and it is because of this dynamic team that Bruce has had the time to return to his true love.

Initially, his return to his artwork was driven by his sheer love of what he loves to paint. He loves the human body - more specifically he loves the FEMALE human body - and it shows in his work. The passion and admiration he feels for women comes through in his work - he loves what he does. It is because of this passion that others have fallen in love with Bruce's work. Artwork that was meant to be "downtime" has taken on a life of its own - he now routinely does work for various comic book and RPG companies.

Bruce's greatest joy is painting and in knowing the people love his work as much as he does. Allow yourself to be captured by the breathtaking and erotic visions he creates.

Heavenly Bodies
The Art of Bruce Colero
Volume One

Book design by Grassy Knoll Studios.

Published by
SQP Inc.
PO Box 248 - Columbus, NJ 08022

Sal Quartuccio & Bob Keenan - Publishers

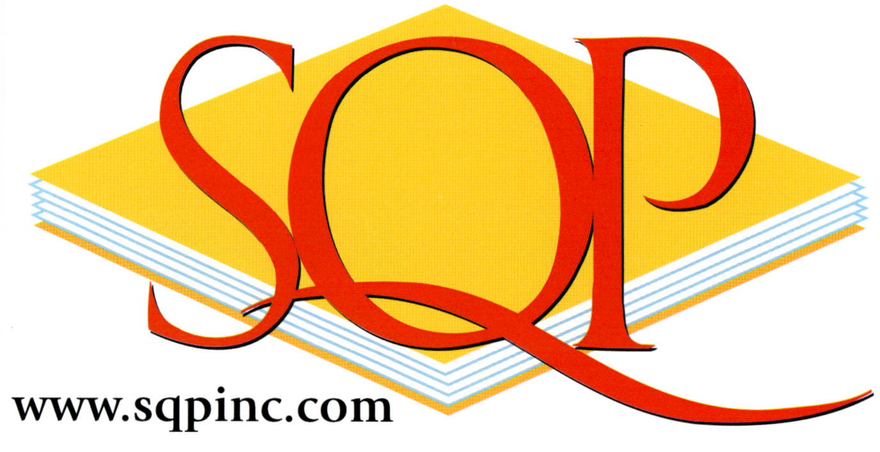

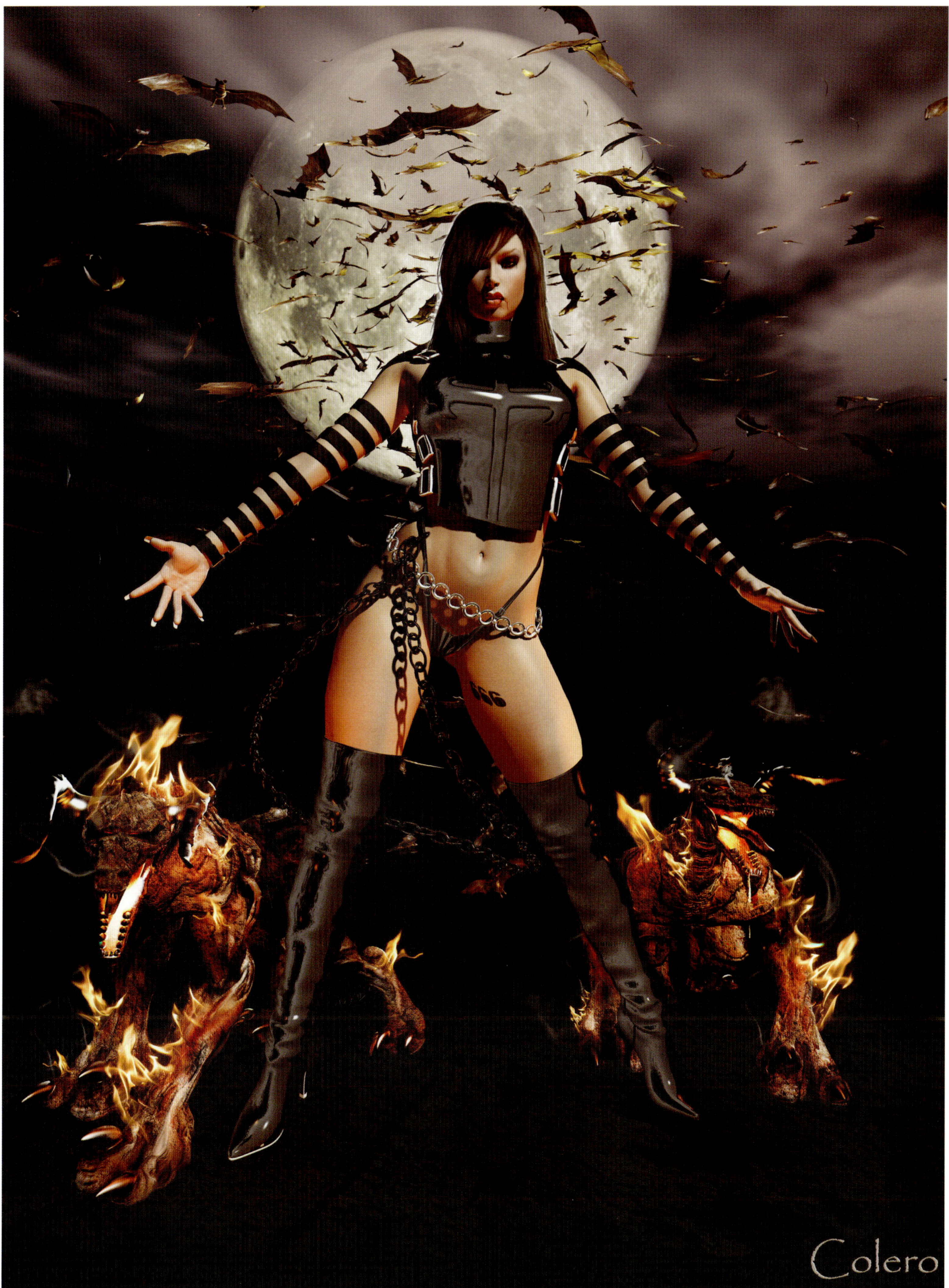

Bad Blood

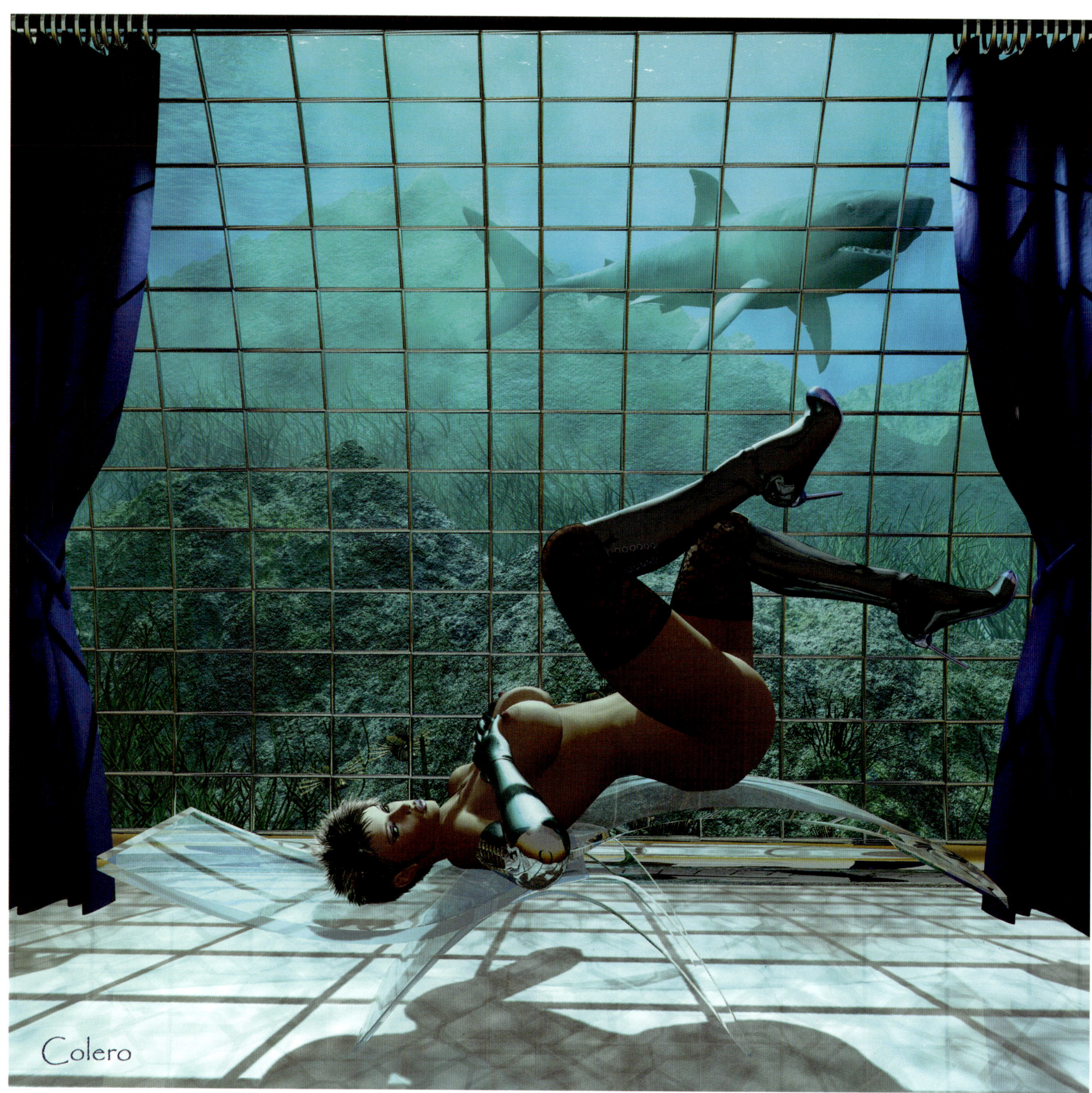

A Room With A View

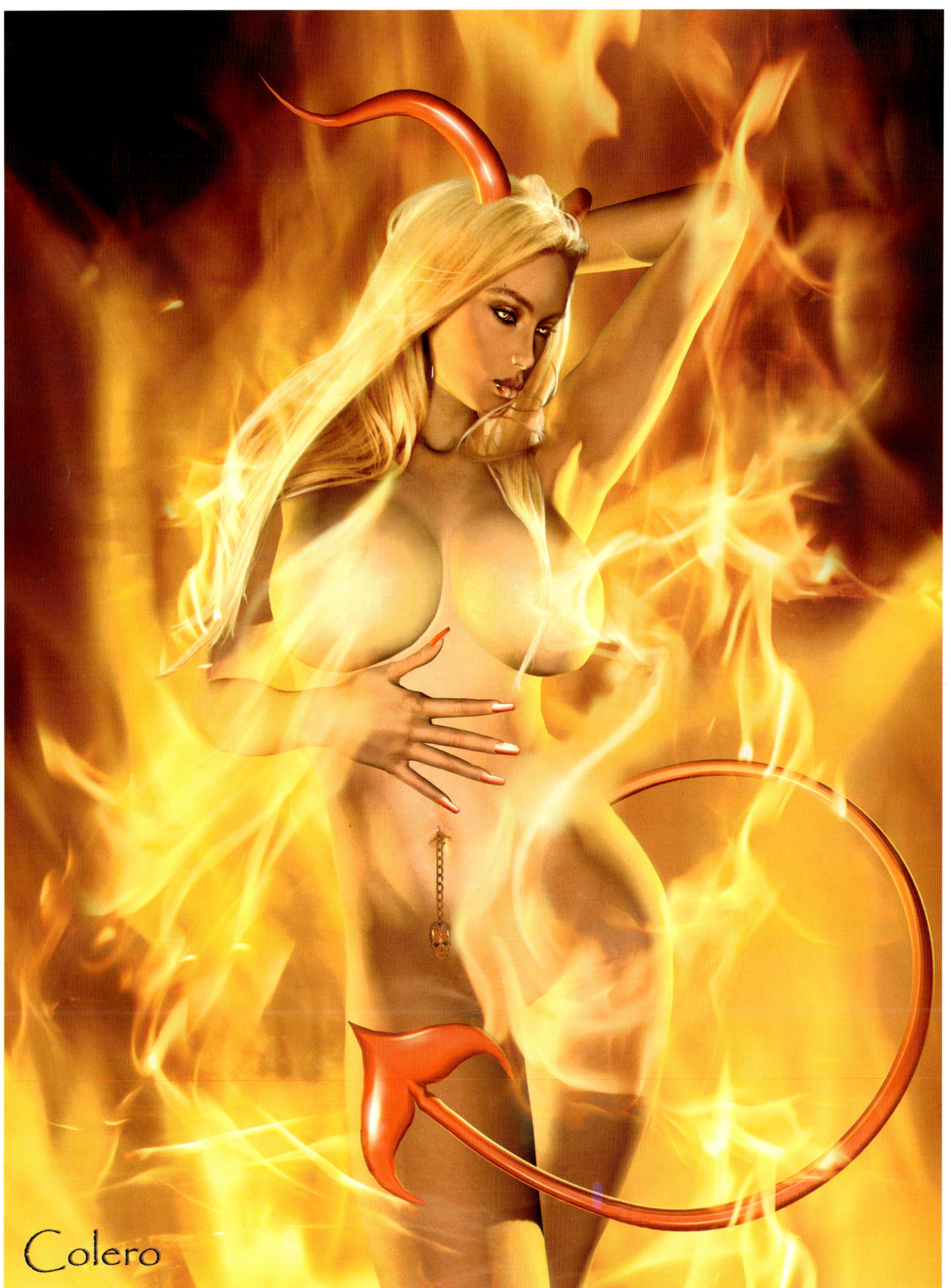

And Lead Us Into...

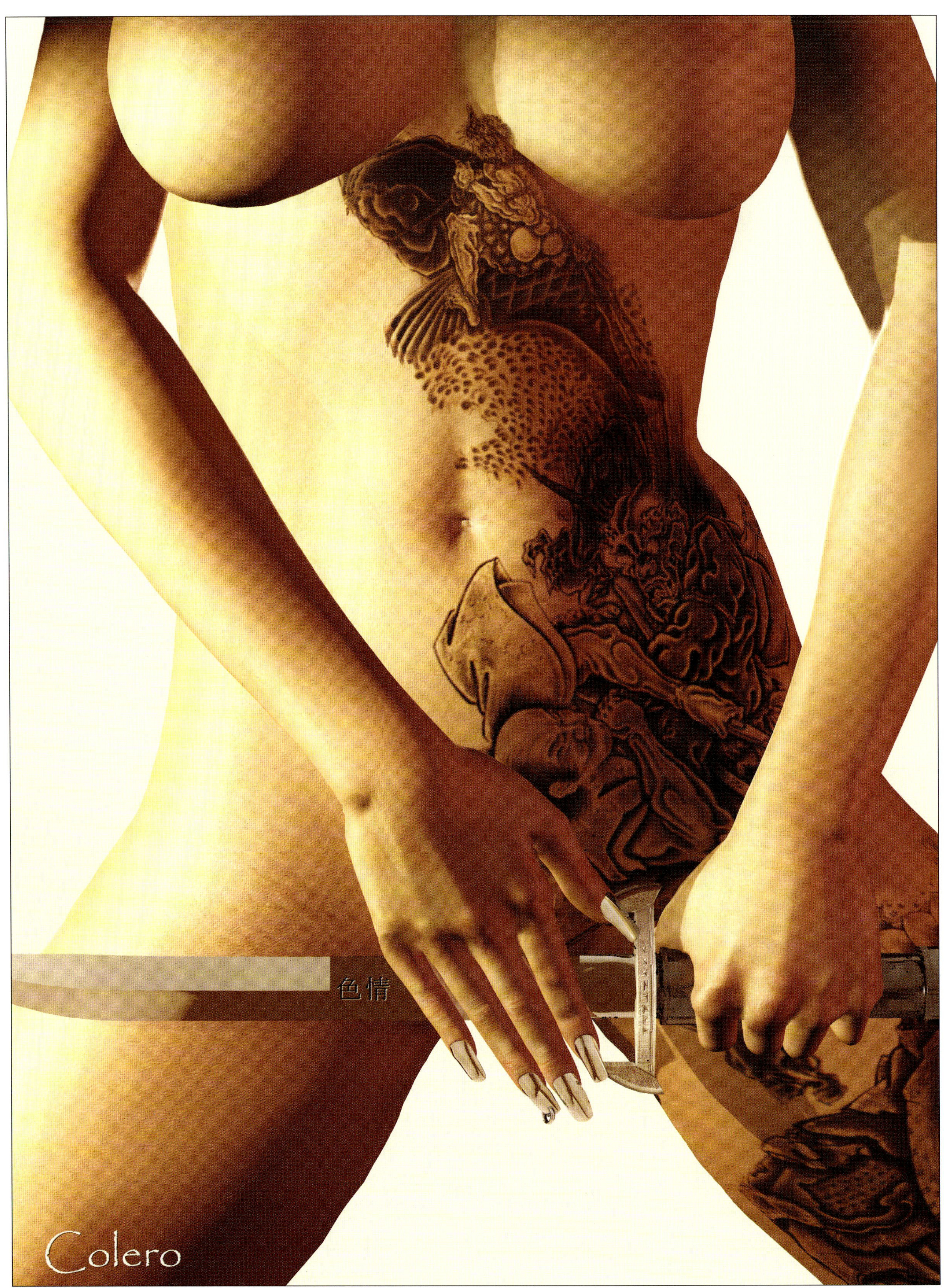

Bushido

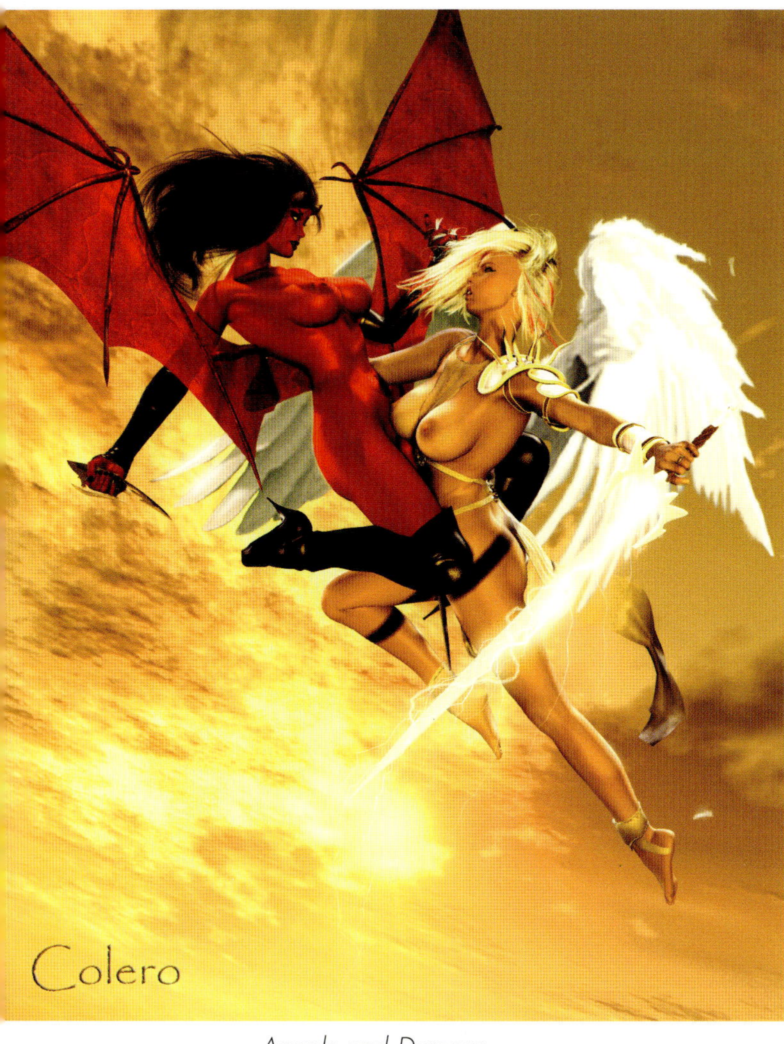

Angels and Demons

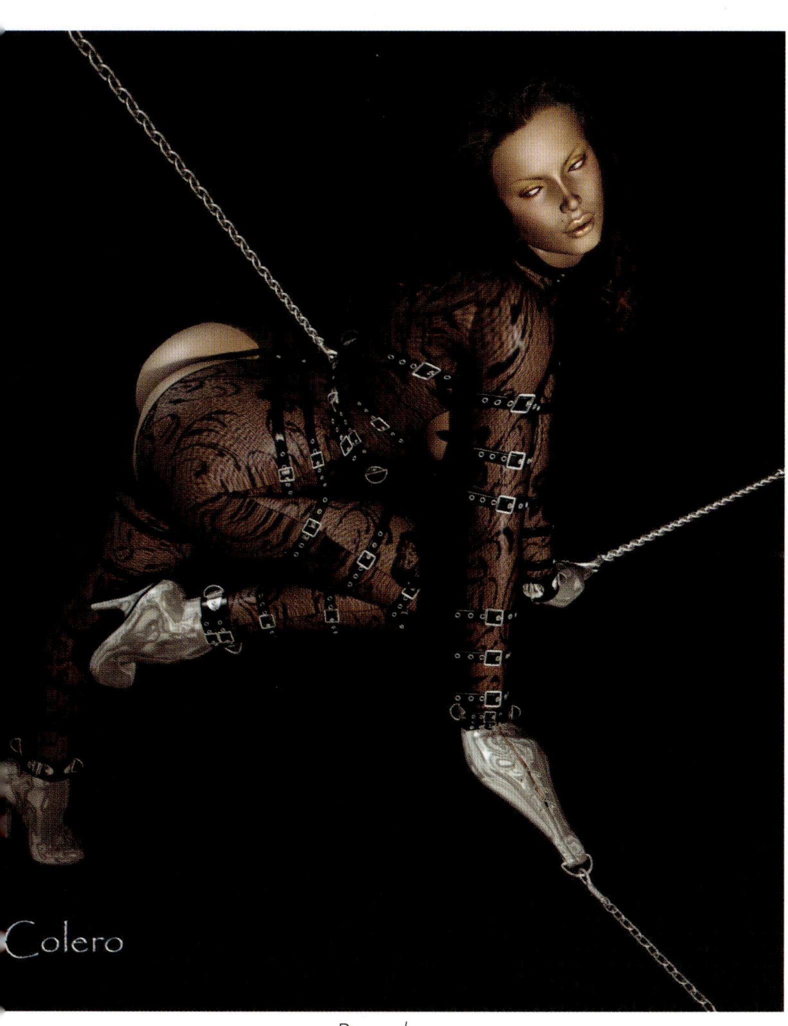

Bound

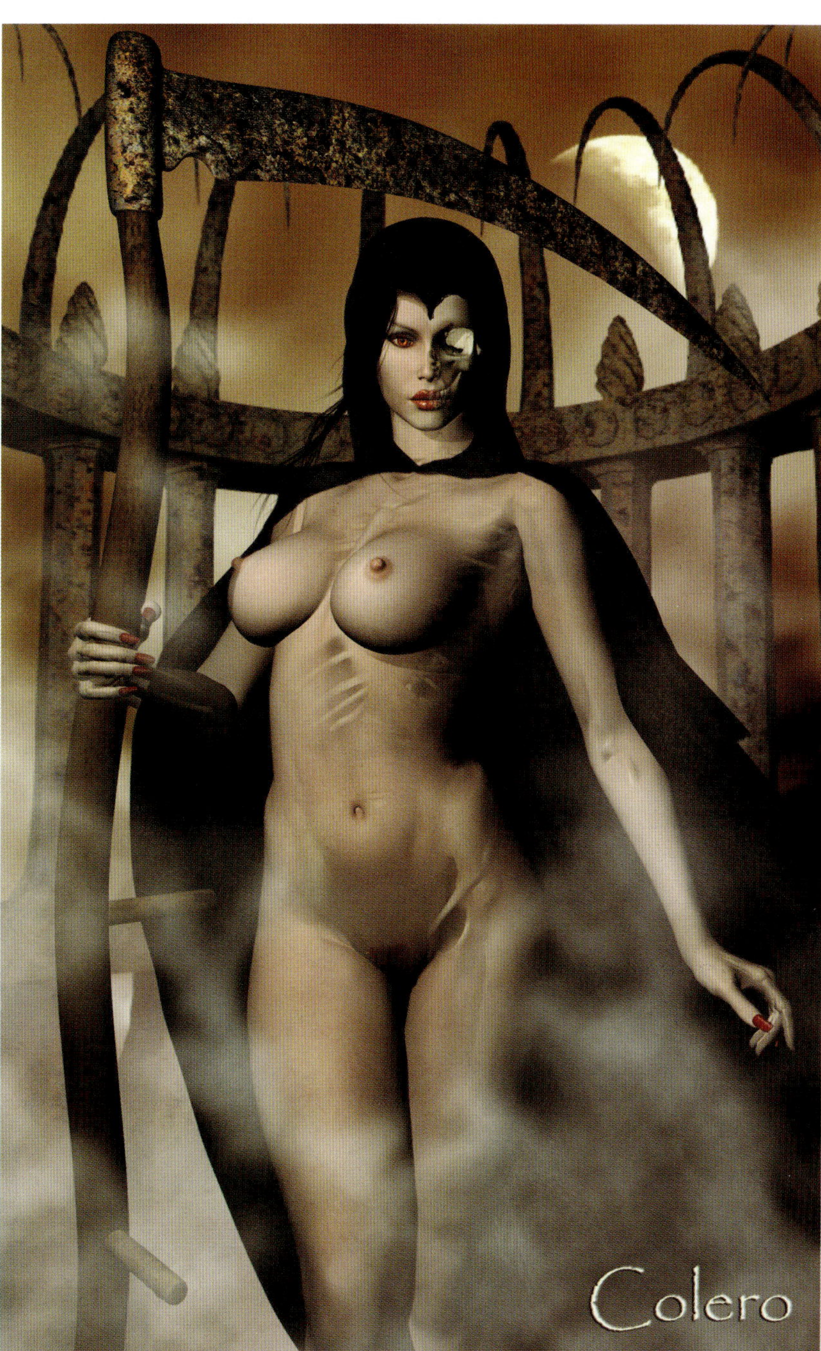

All Men Are Mine...

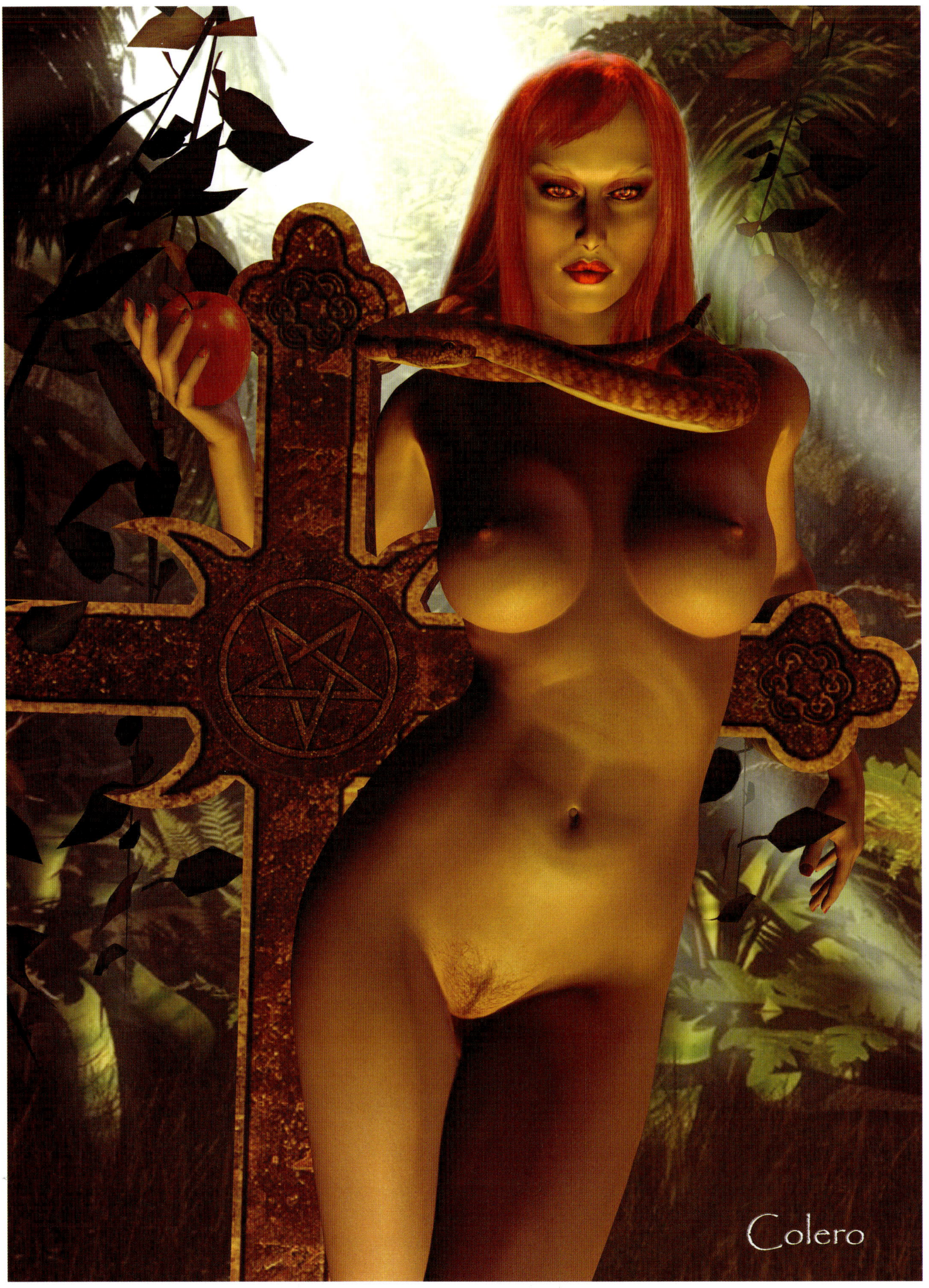

Original Sin

Opposite Page
Almost Heaven

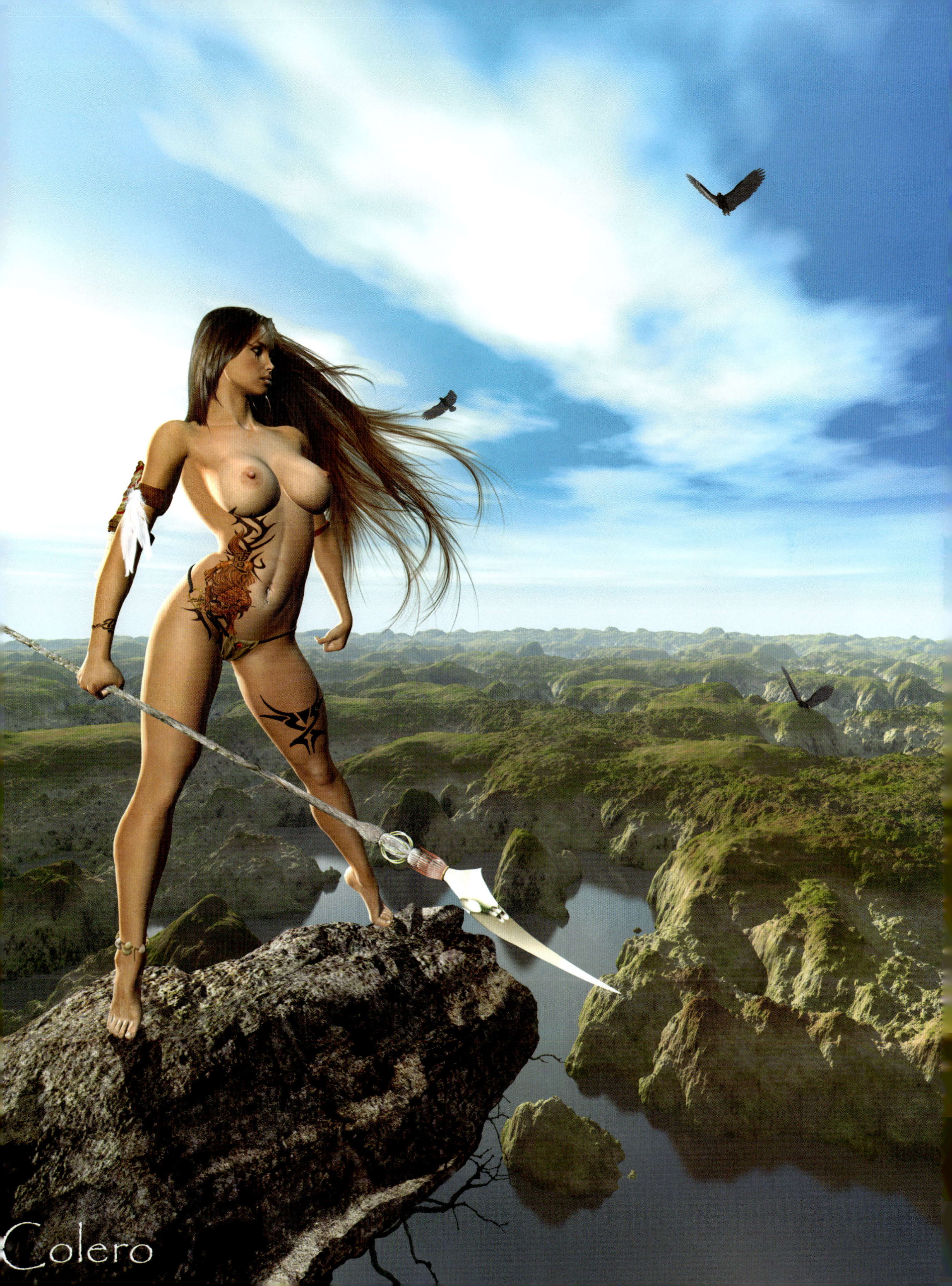
Colero

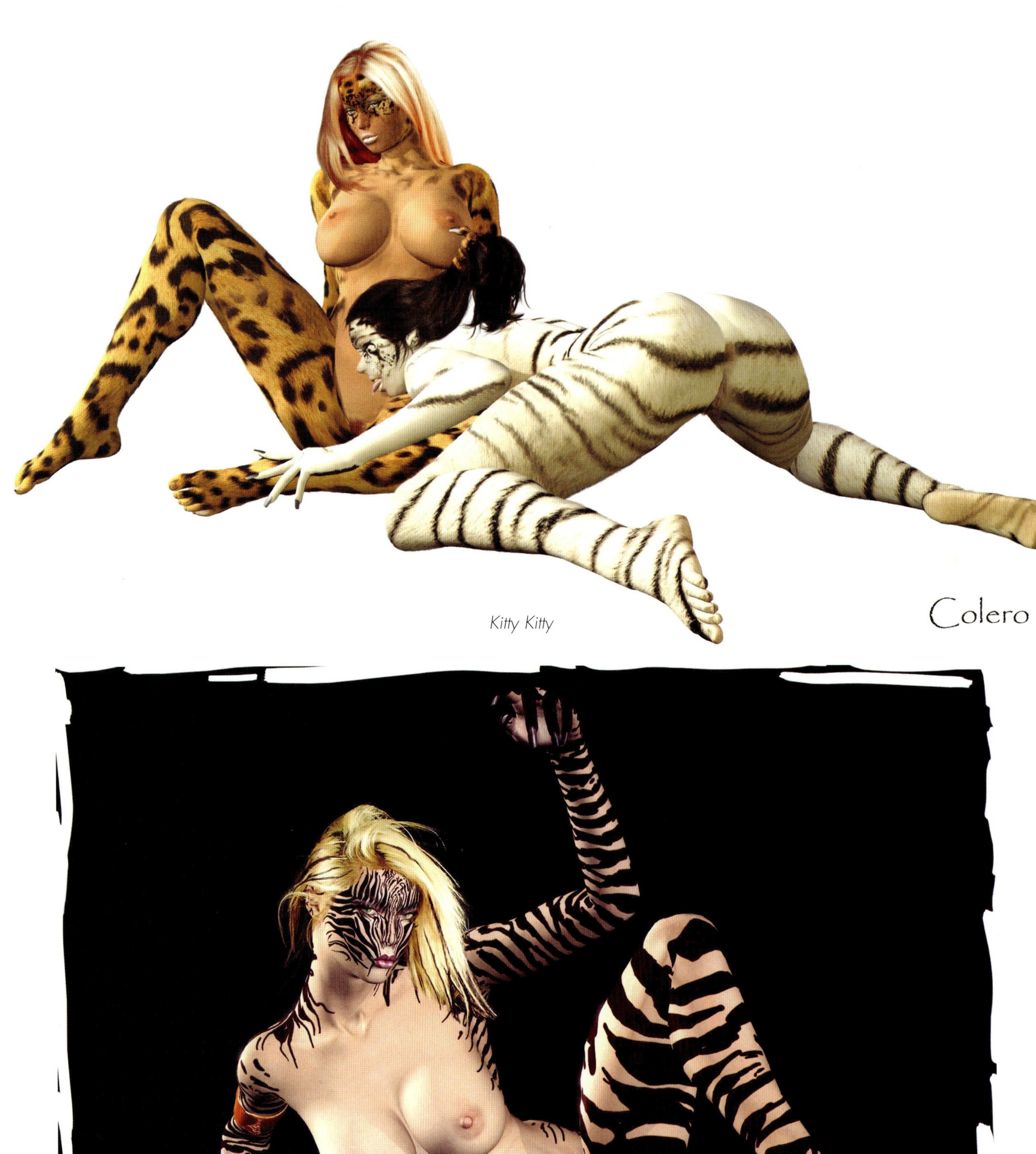

Kitty Kitty

Zebrina

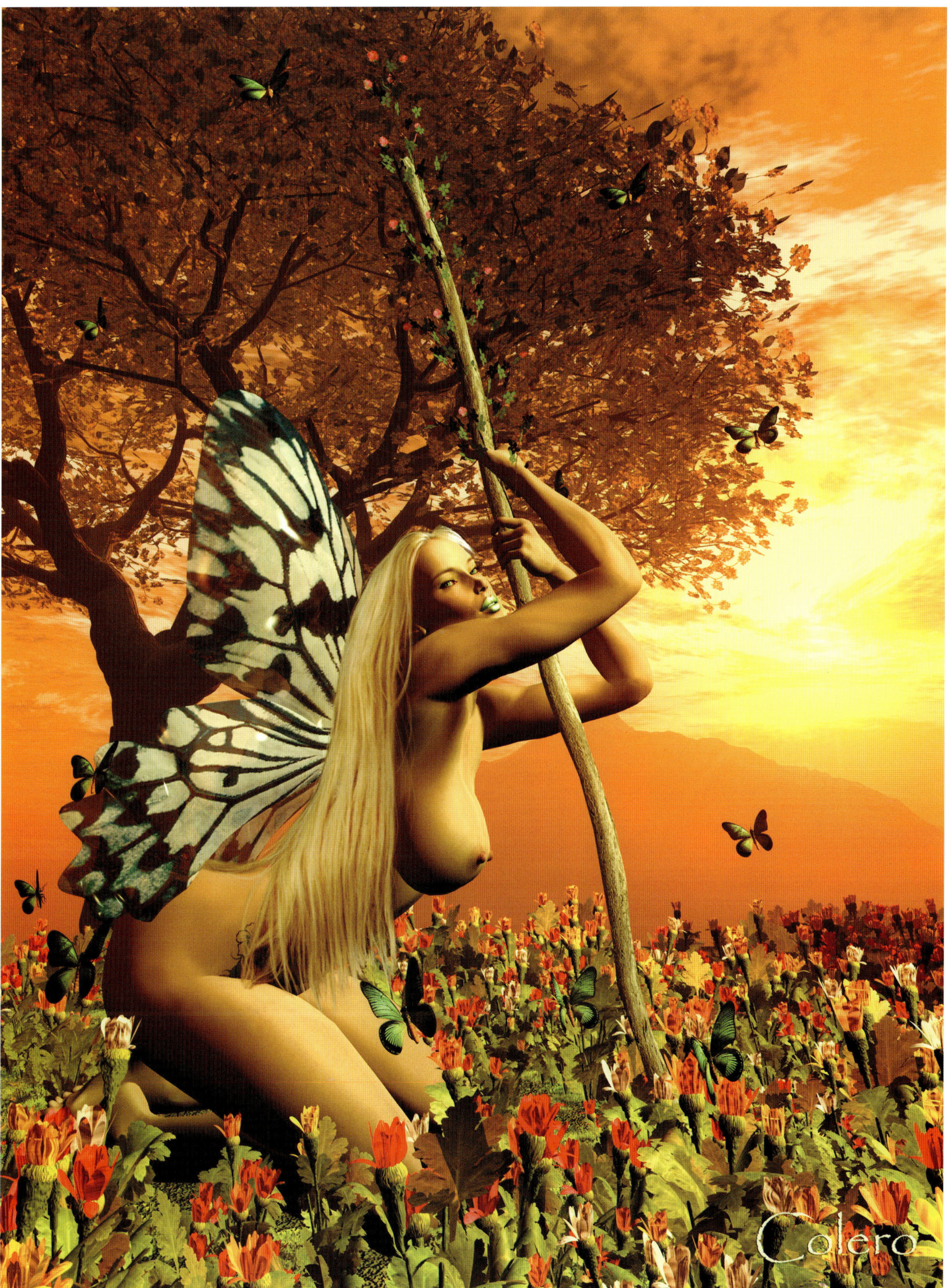

Nymph

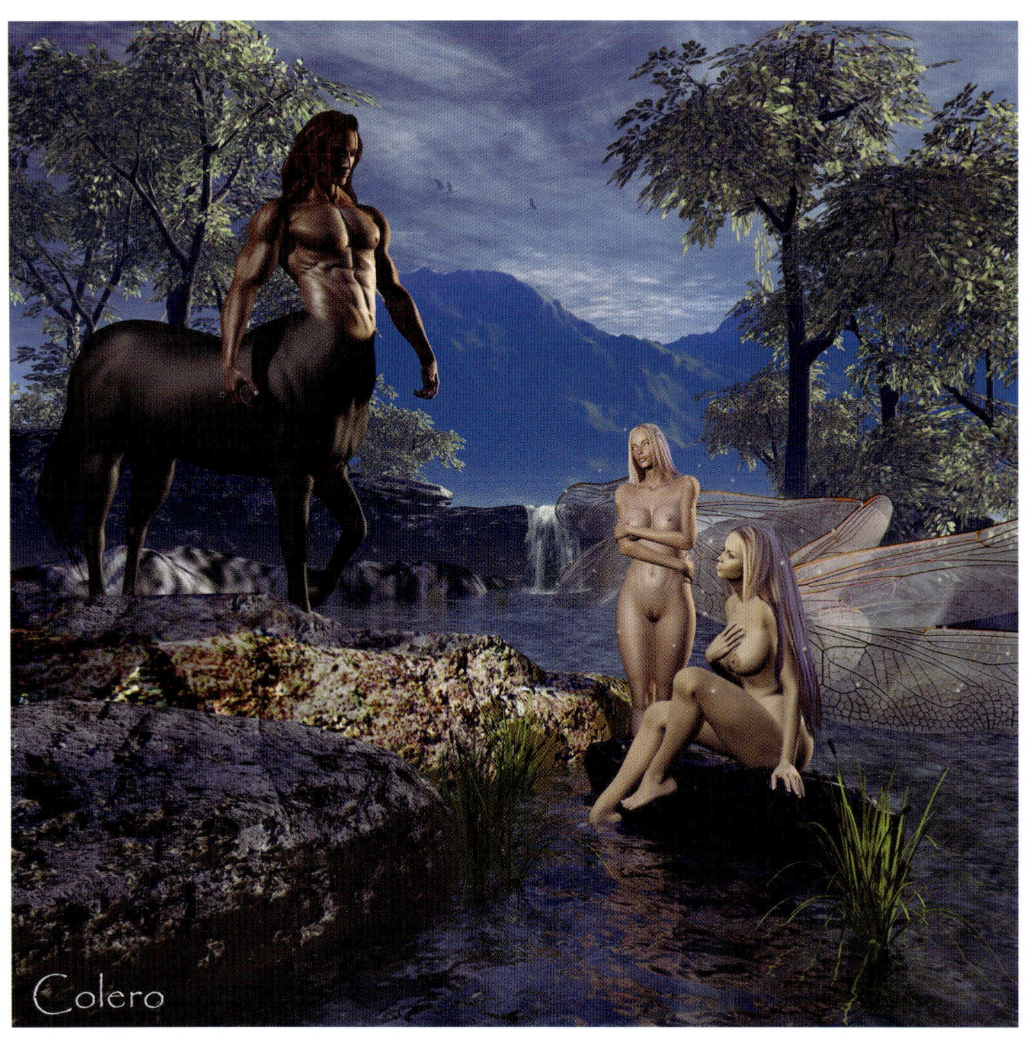

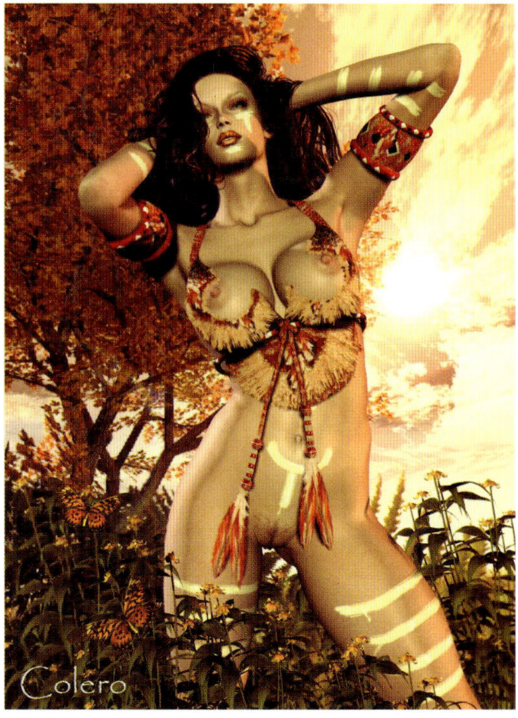

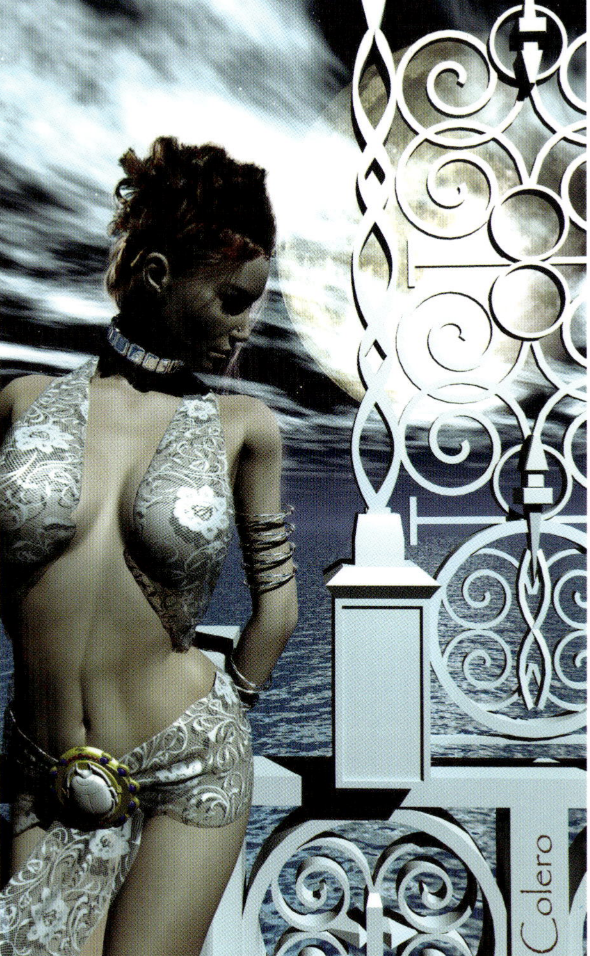

Clockwise from upper left:
Of Myth And Magic
Morning Sun
Wood Nymph
Solitude

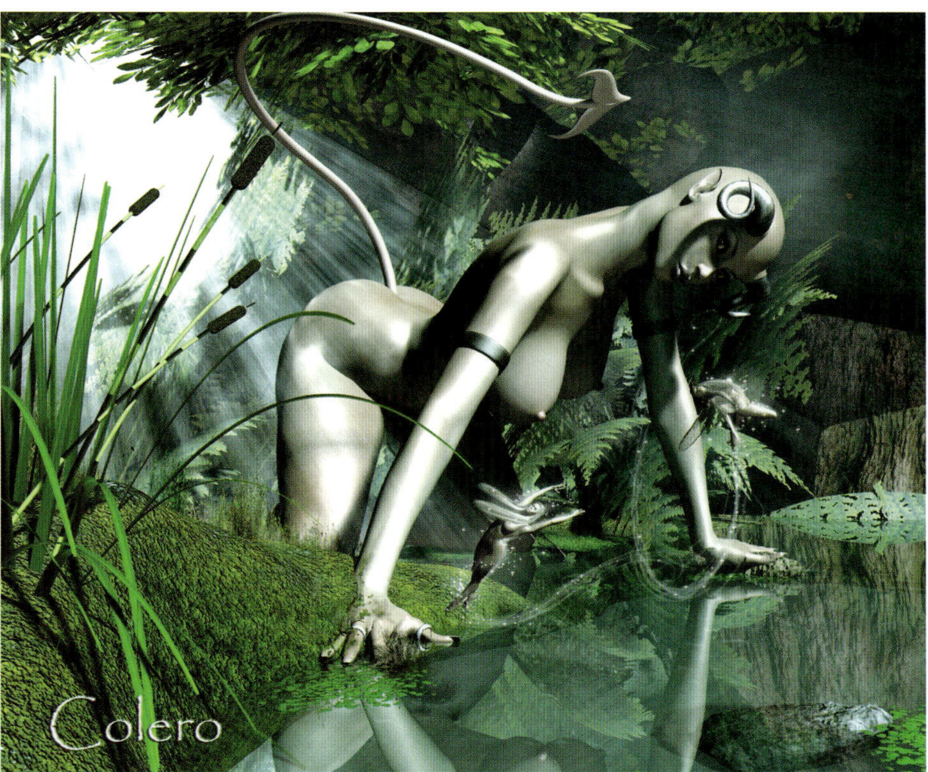

Opposite Page
The Humber River

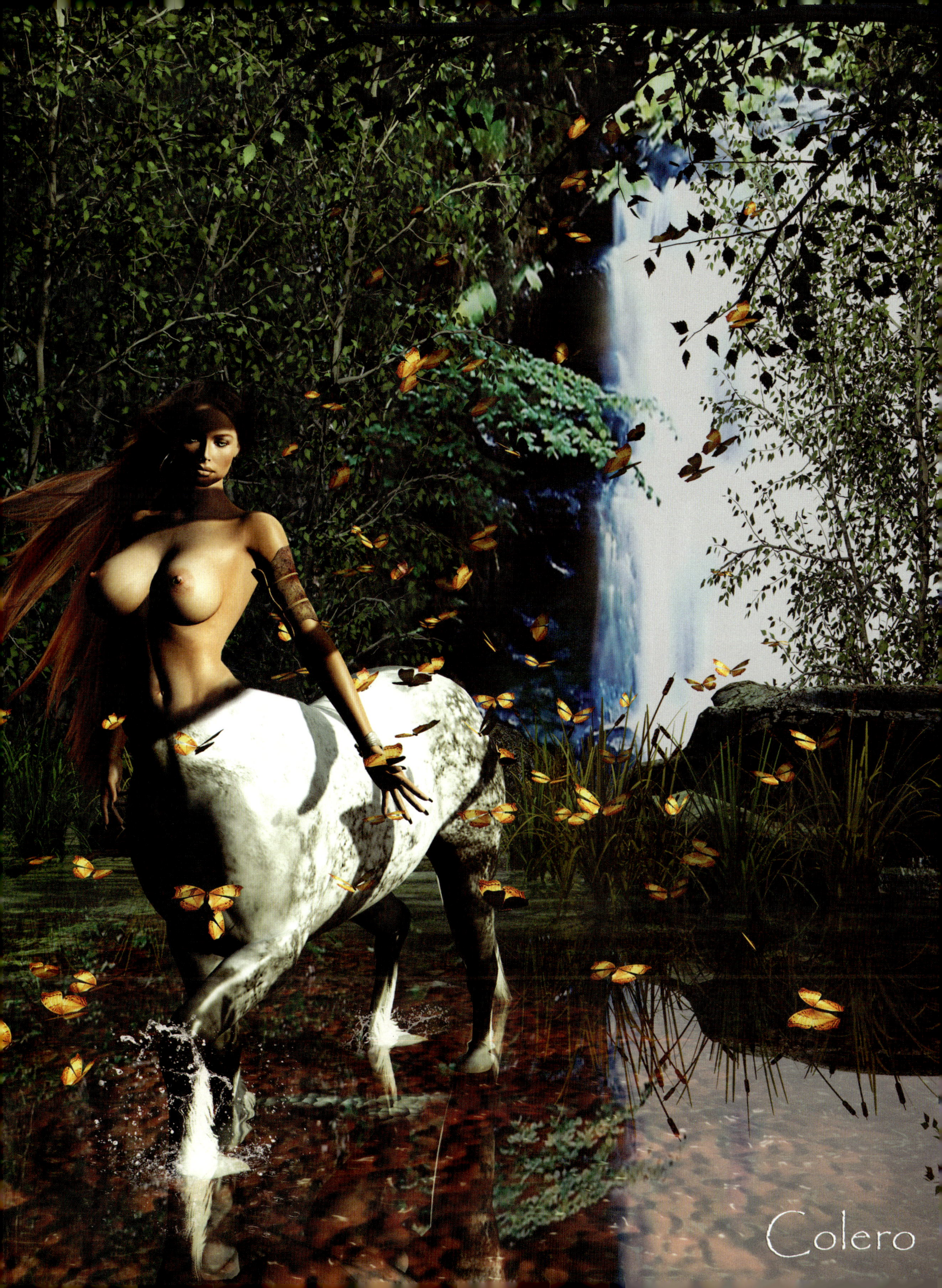
Colero

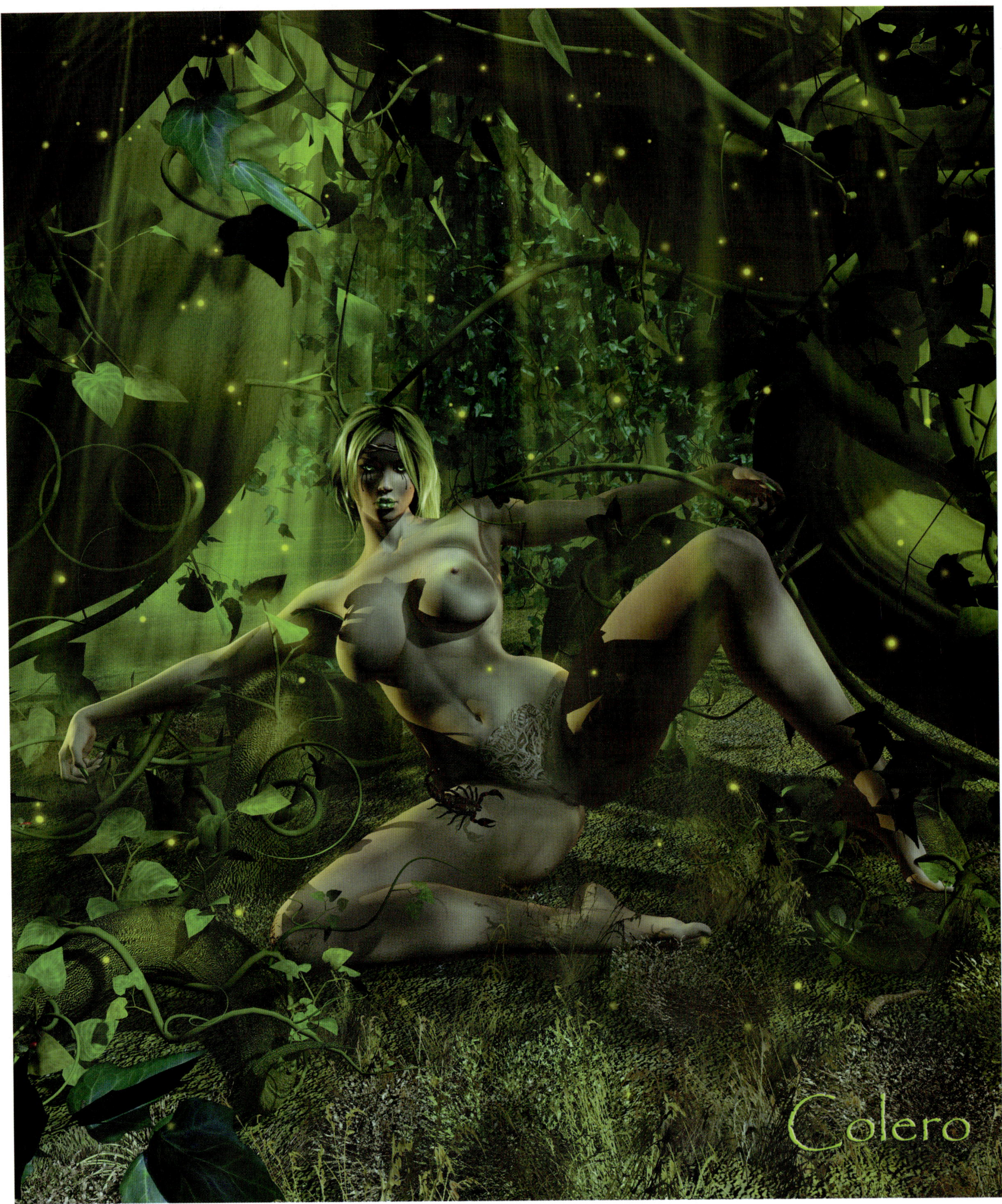

Mother Nature

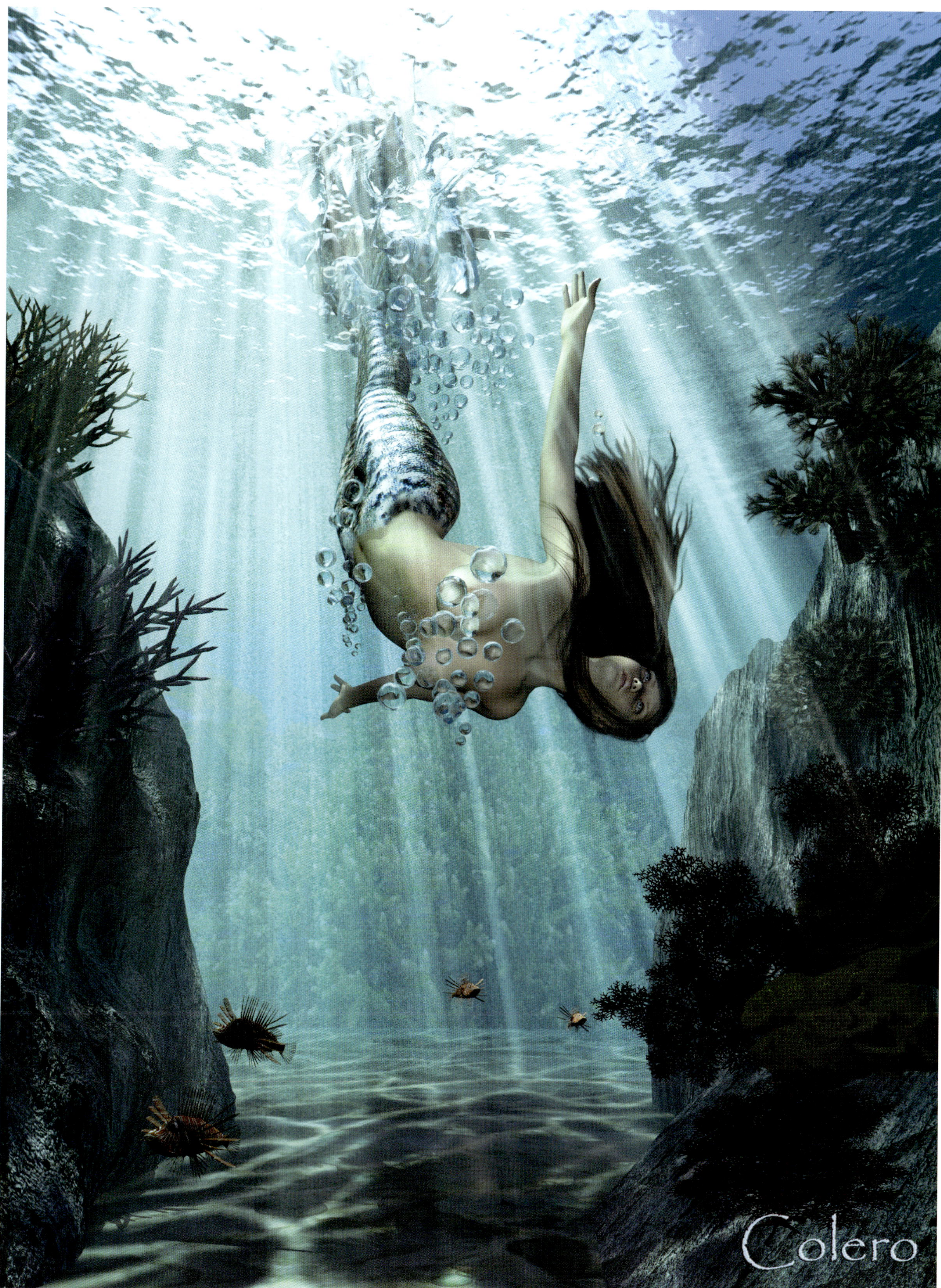

The Red Sea

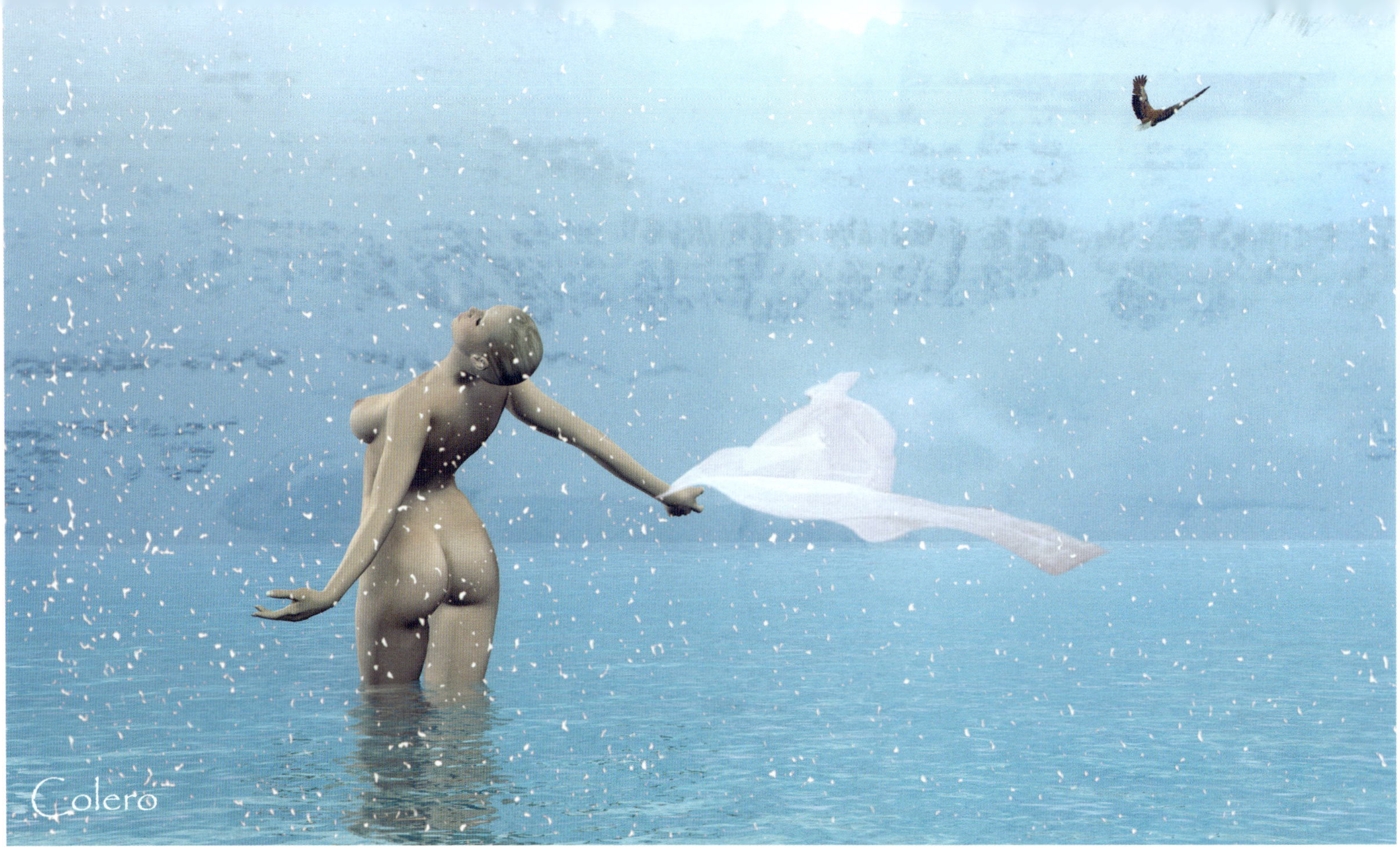

Colero

Born of Winter

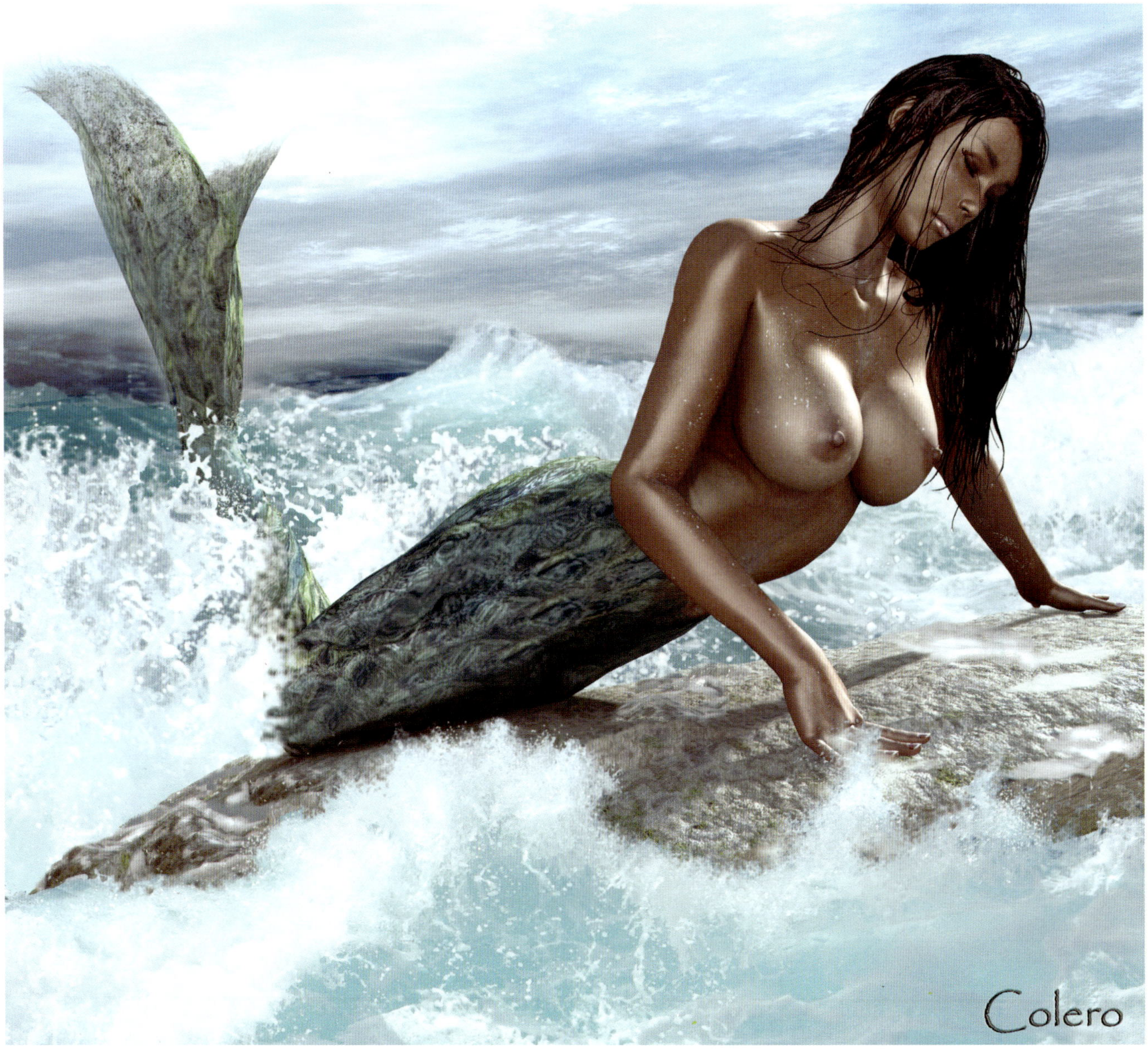

Colero

Mermaid

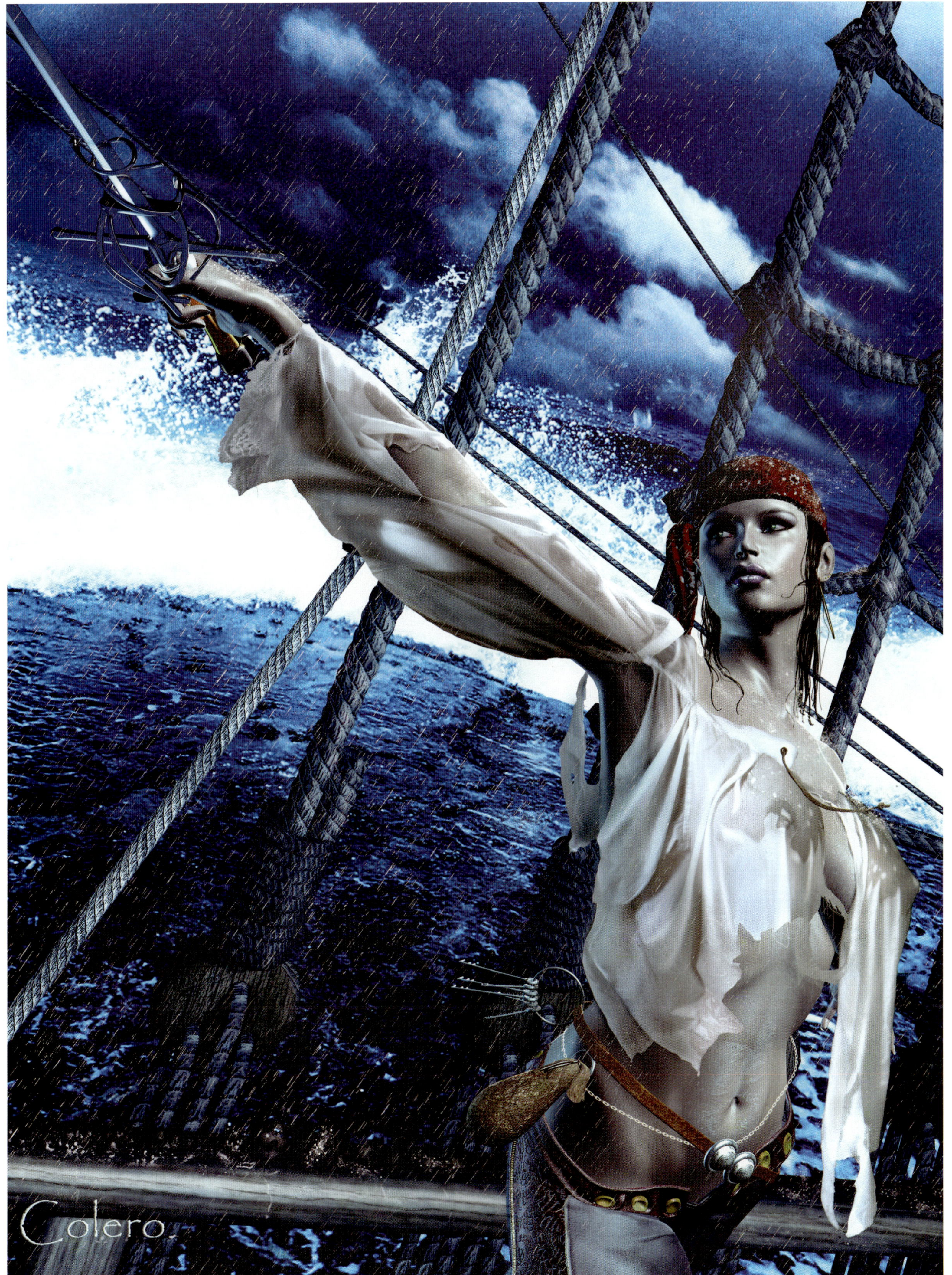

Corsair

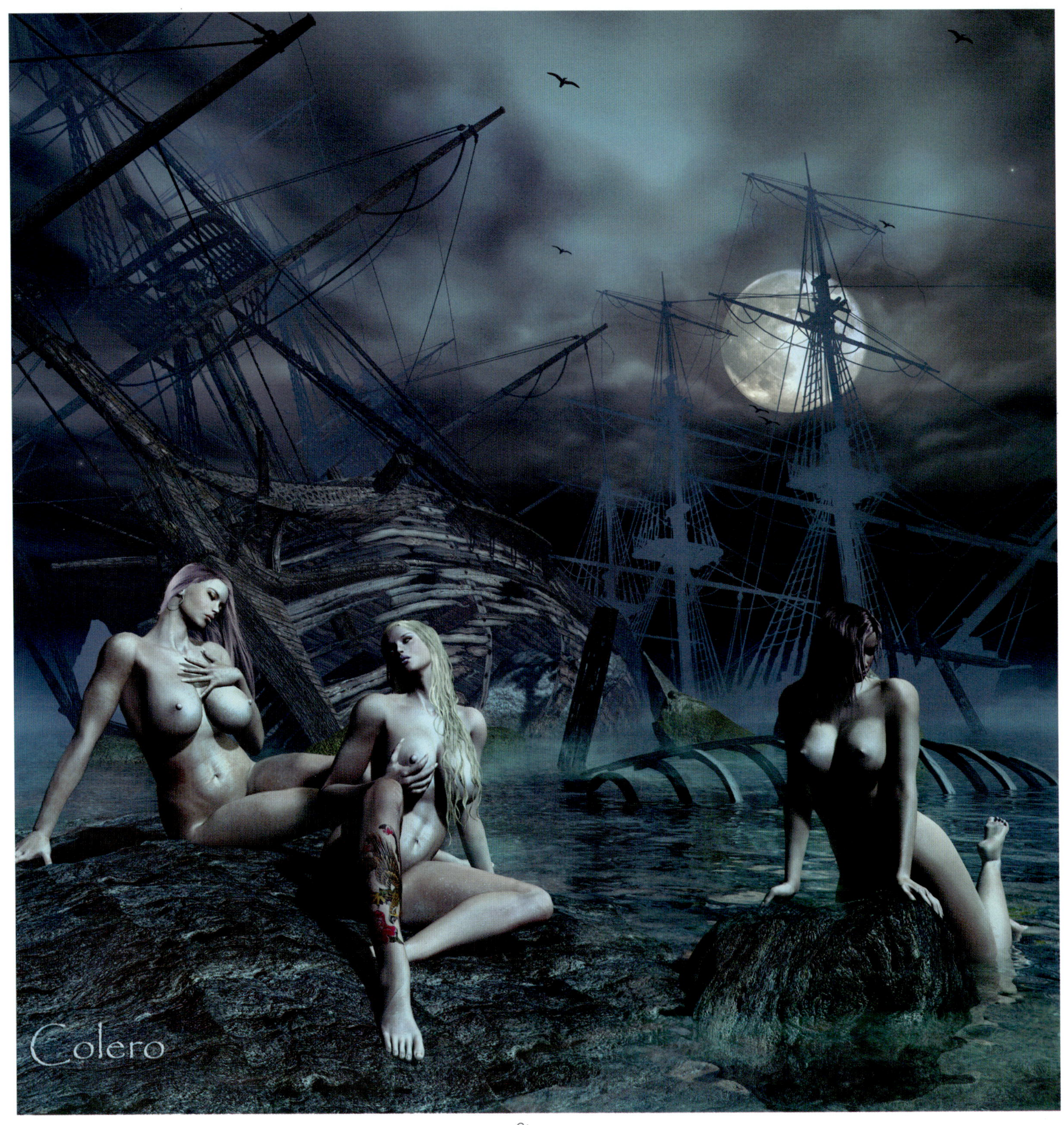

Sirens

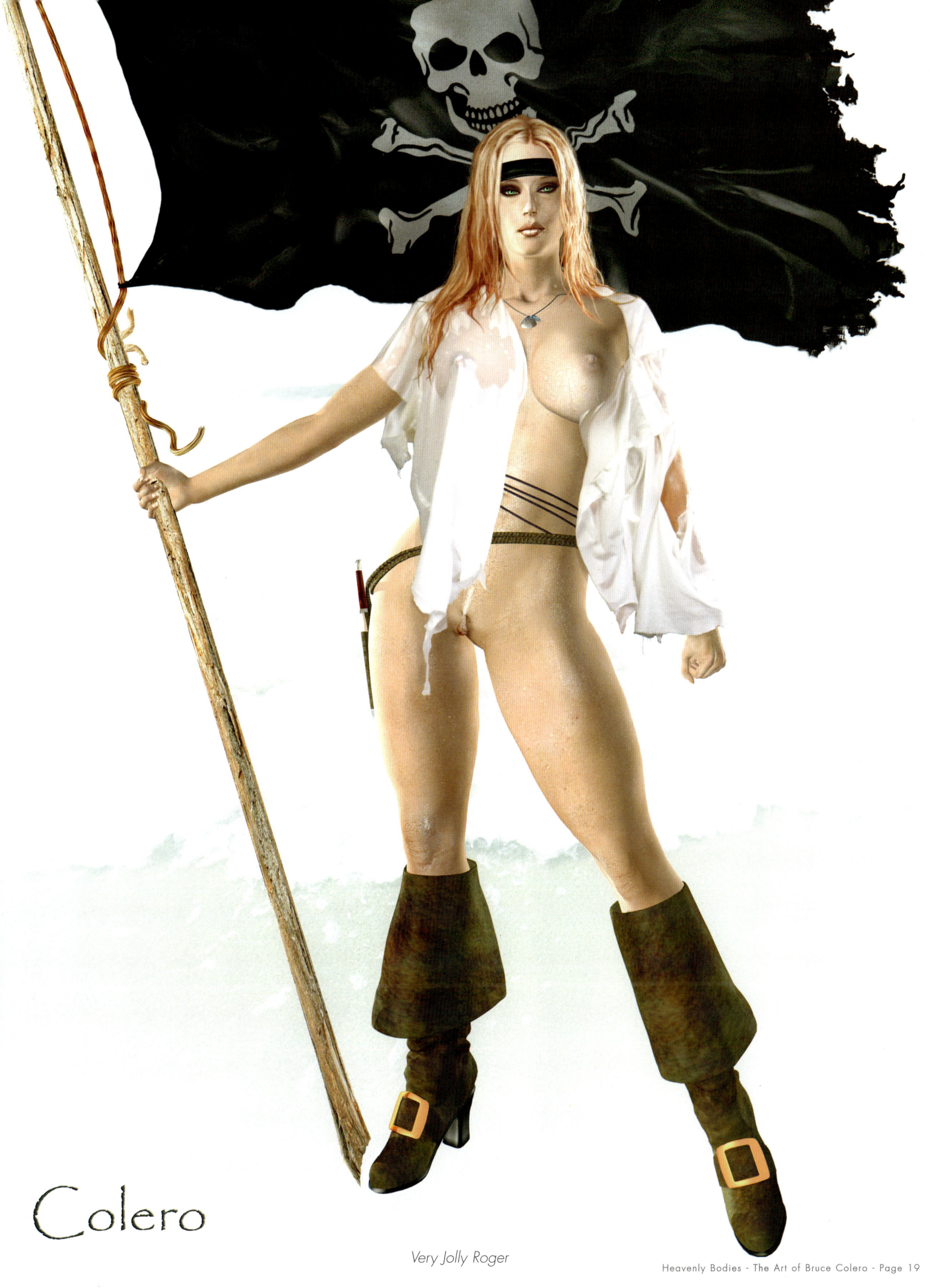

Very Jolly Roger

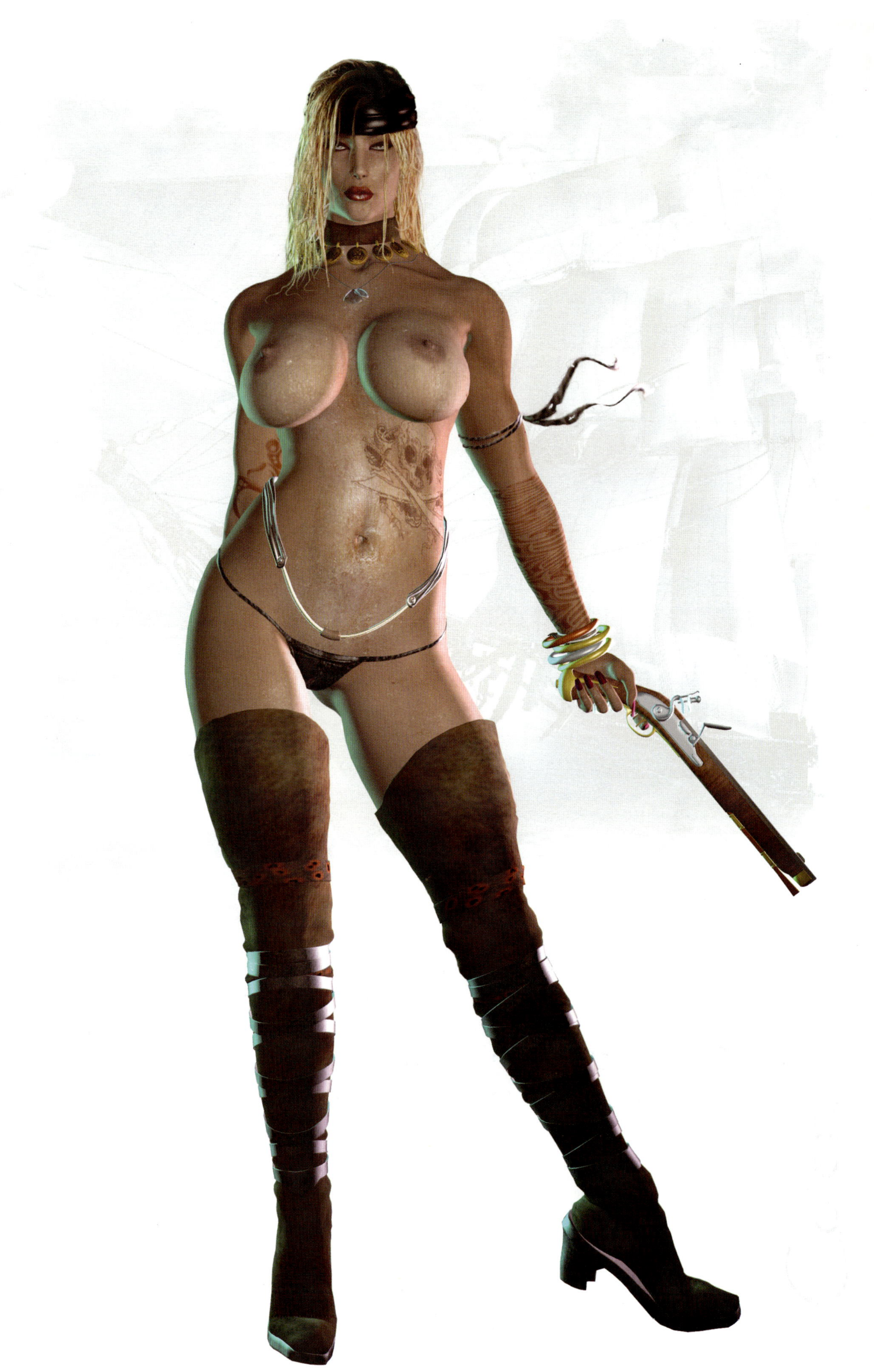

Precious Booty

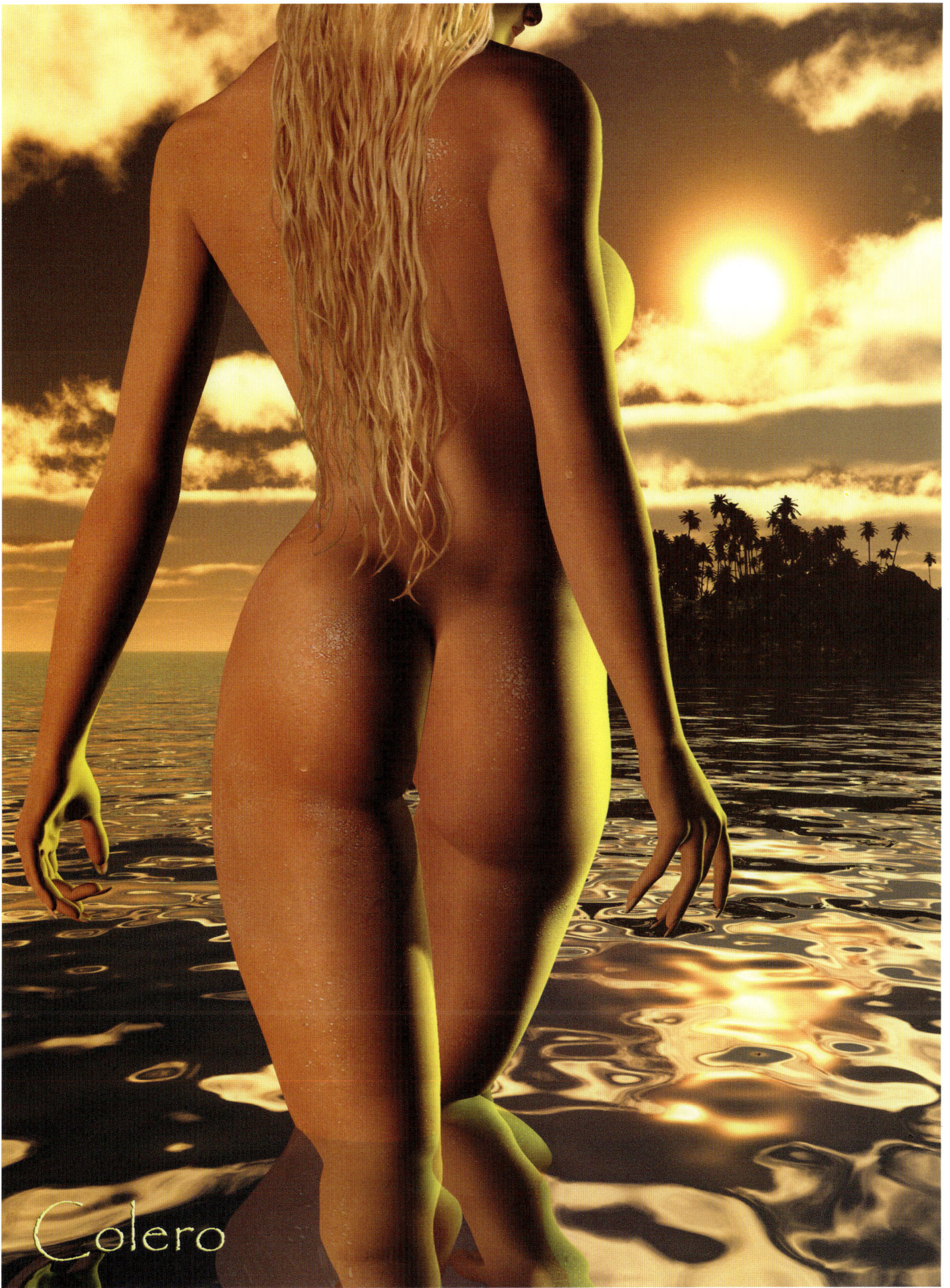

Rio

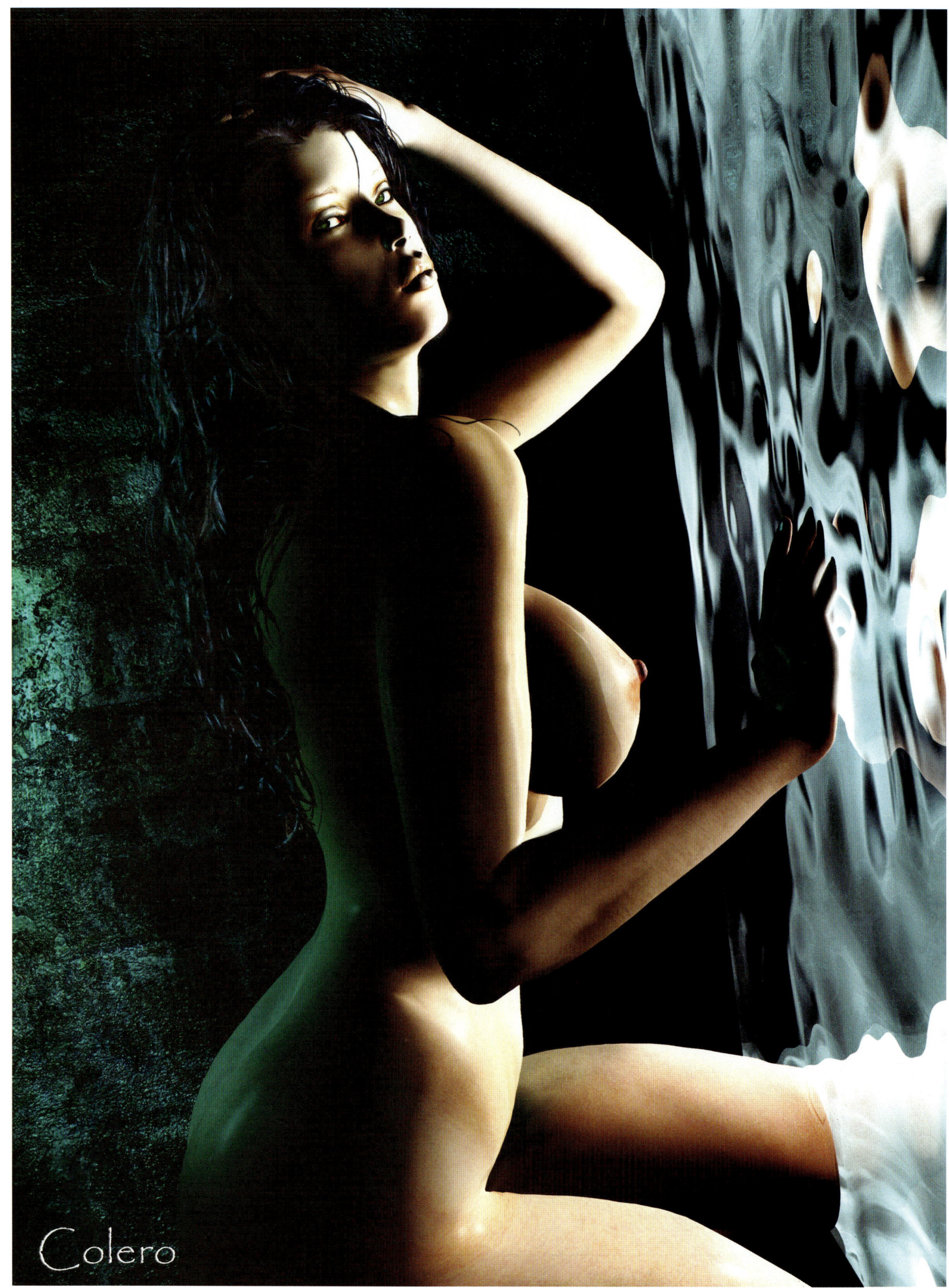

Reflections of...

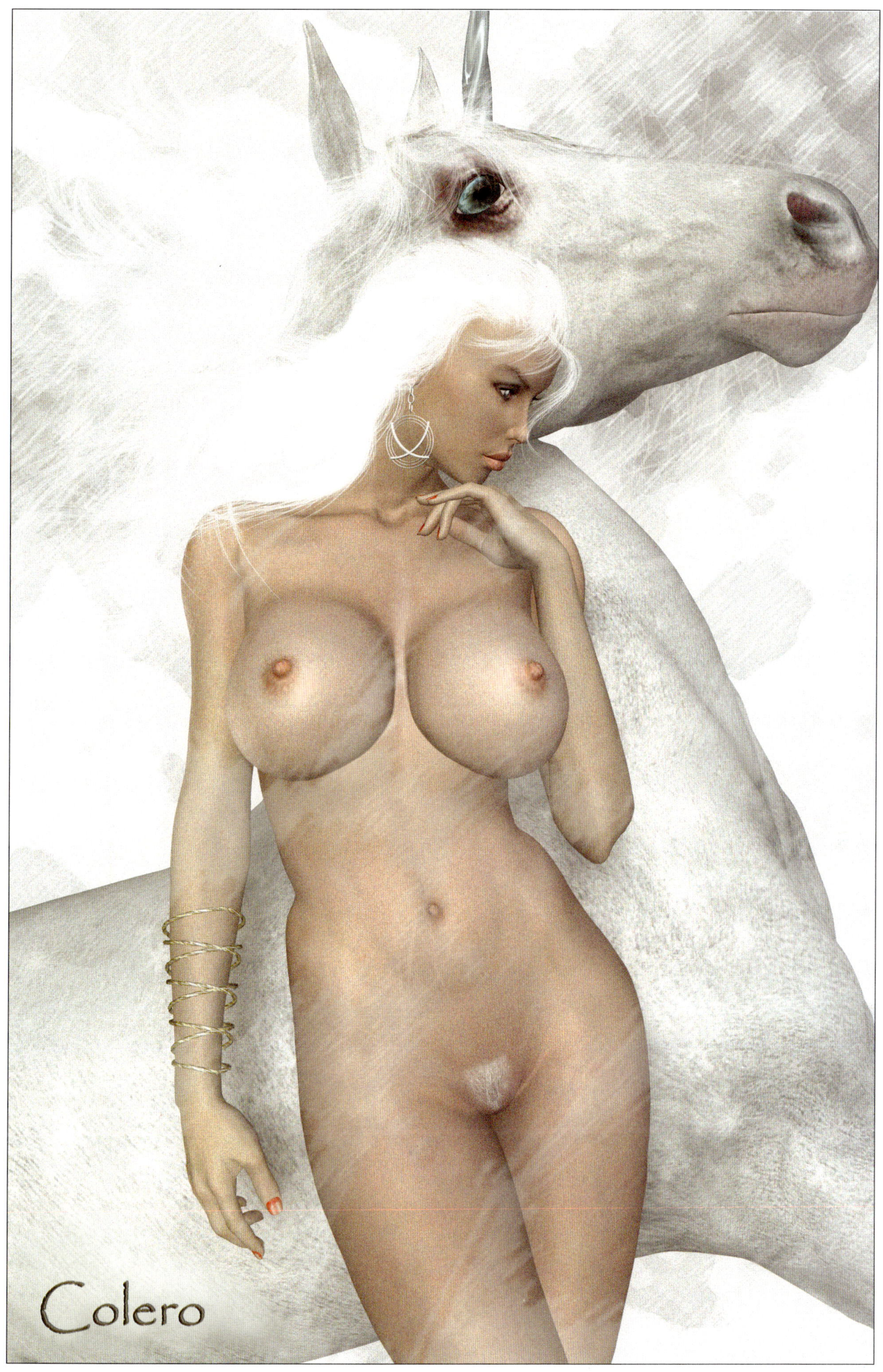

Pure

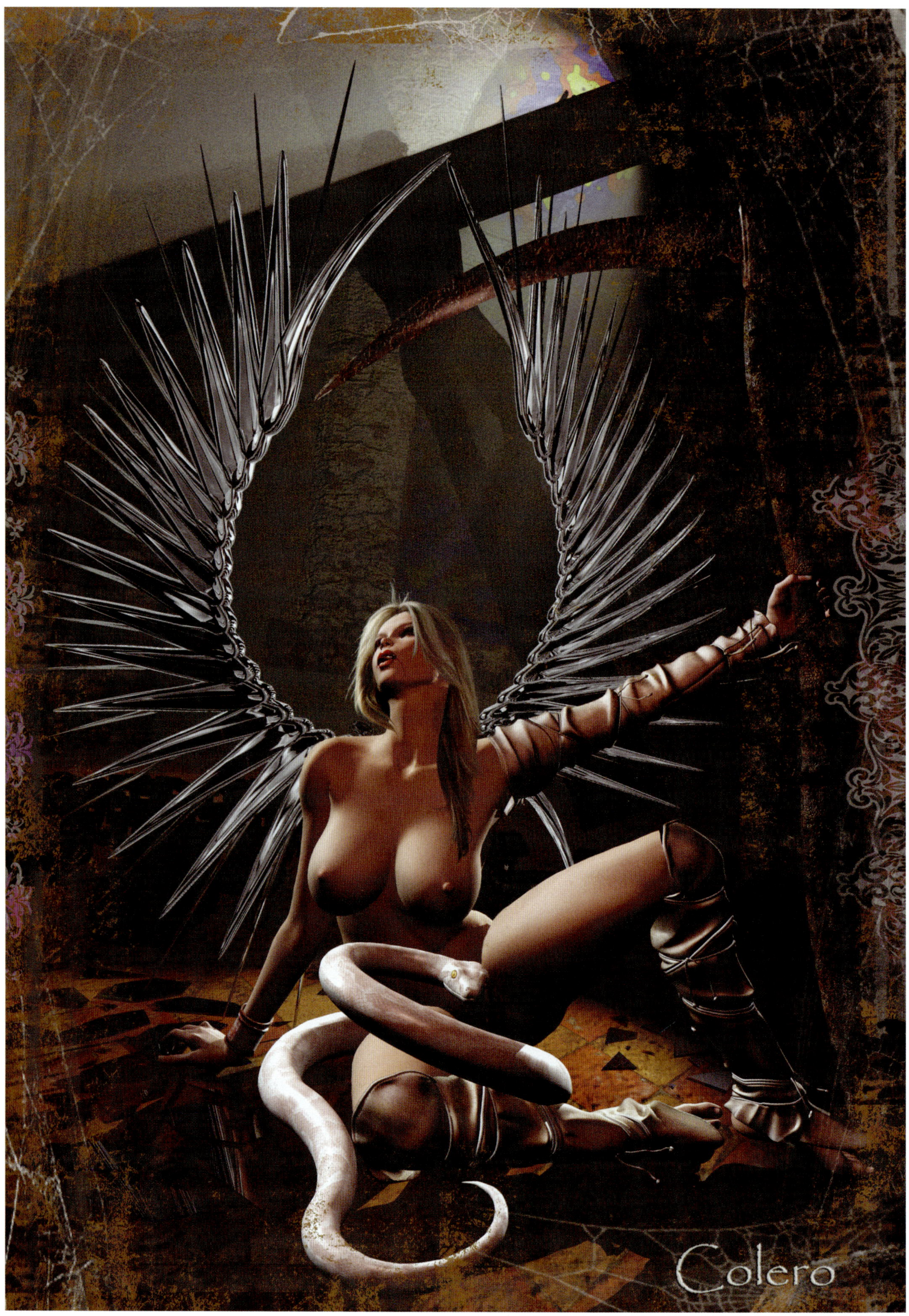

Sanctuary

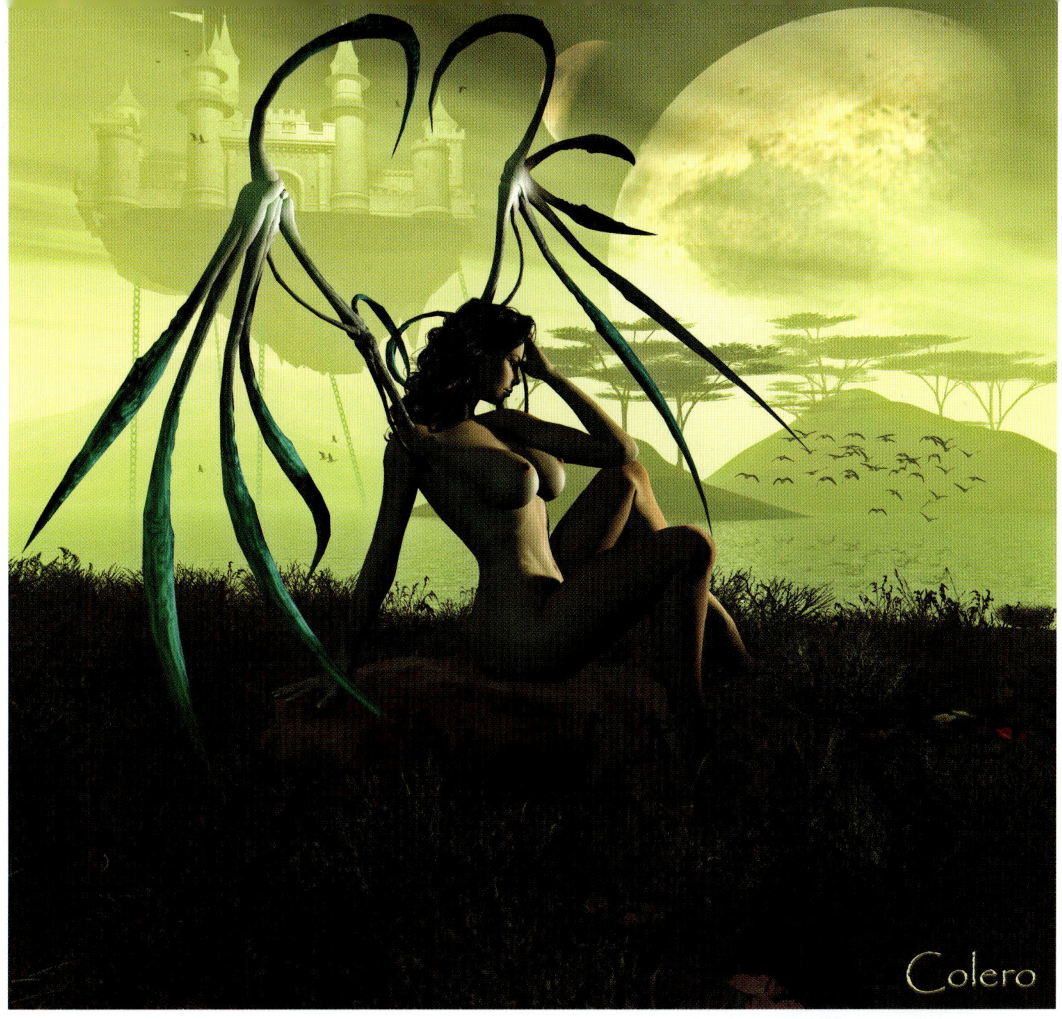

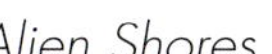

Alien Shores

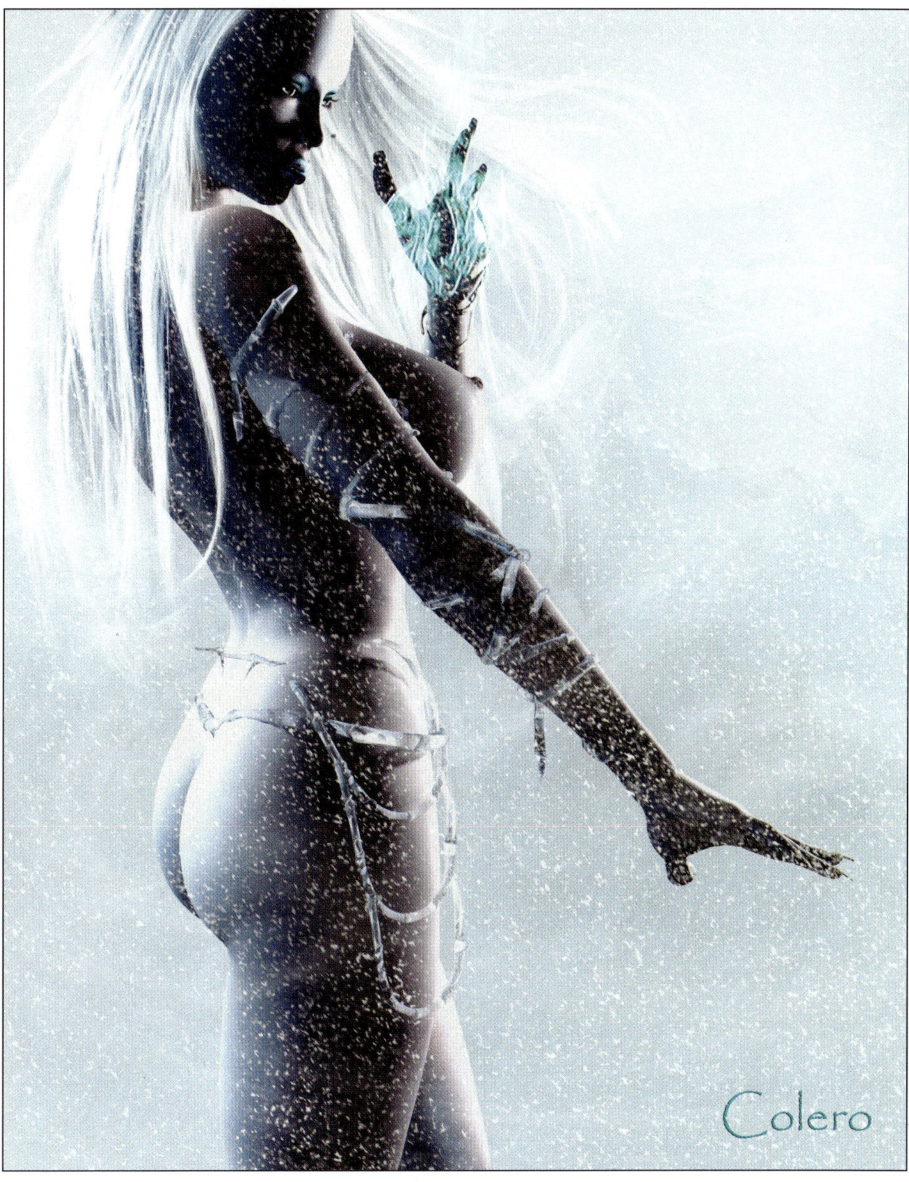

Winter's Kiss

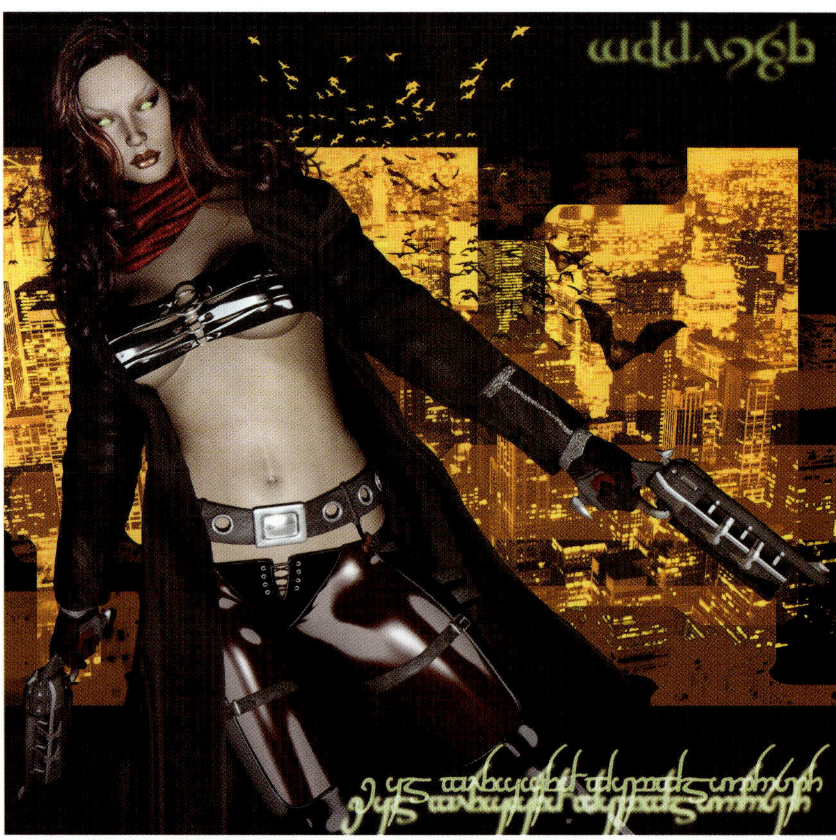

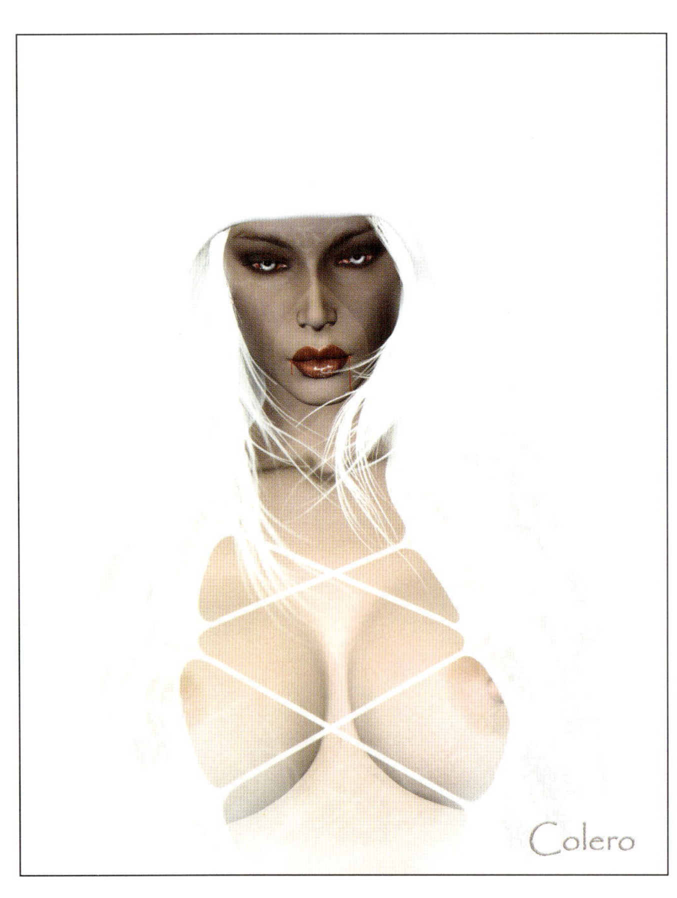
Colero

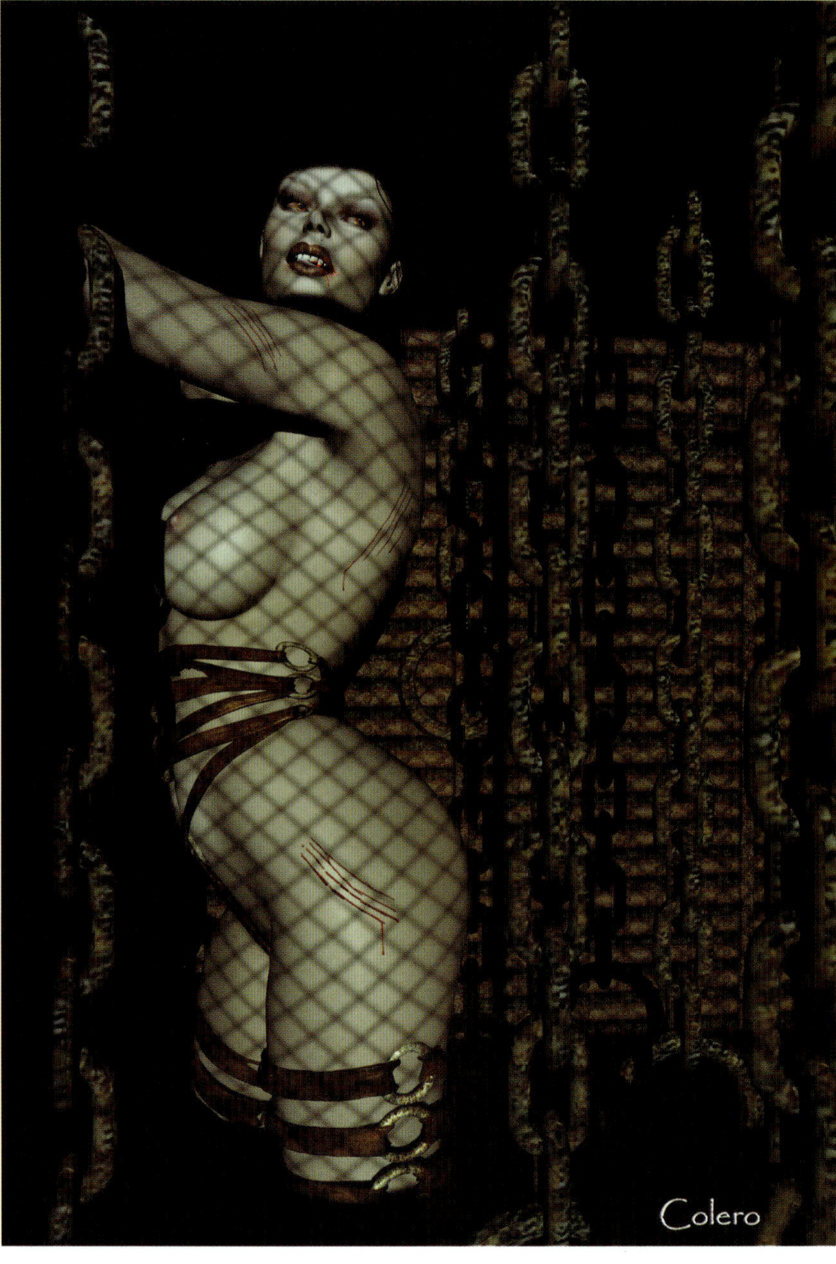
Colero

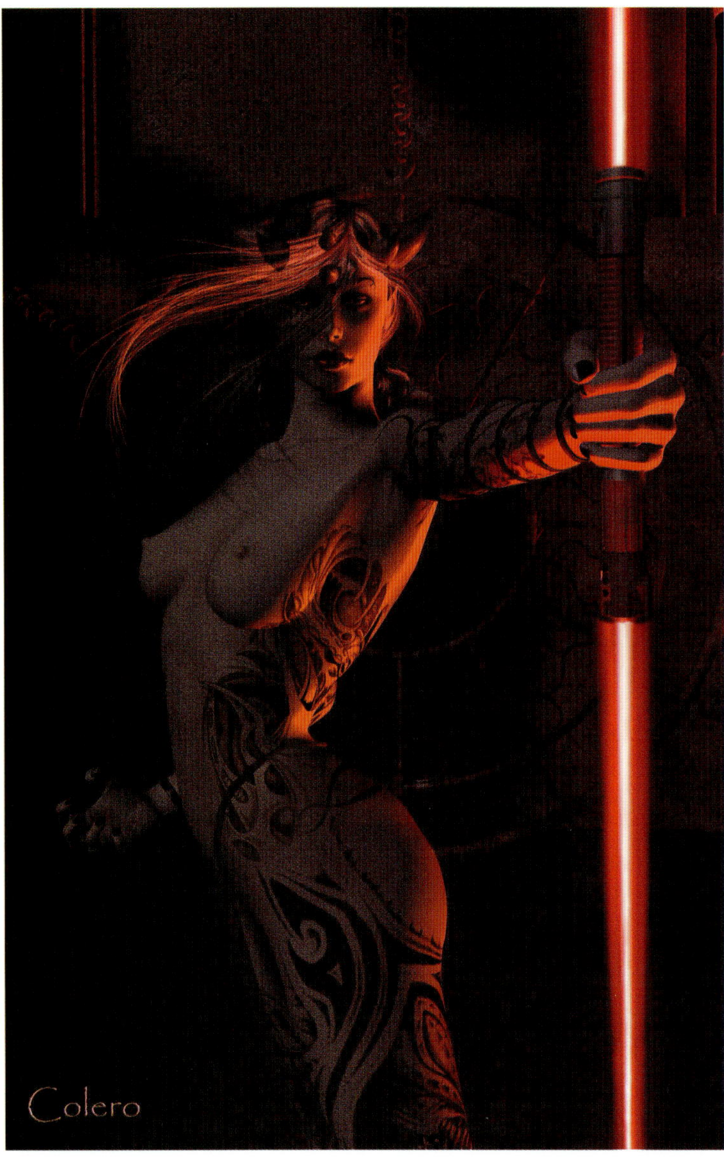
Colero

Opposite Page
Clockwise from upper left:
Unholy
Witchhunter
The Hunger
Sith

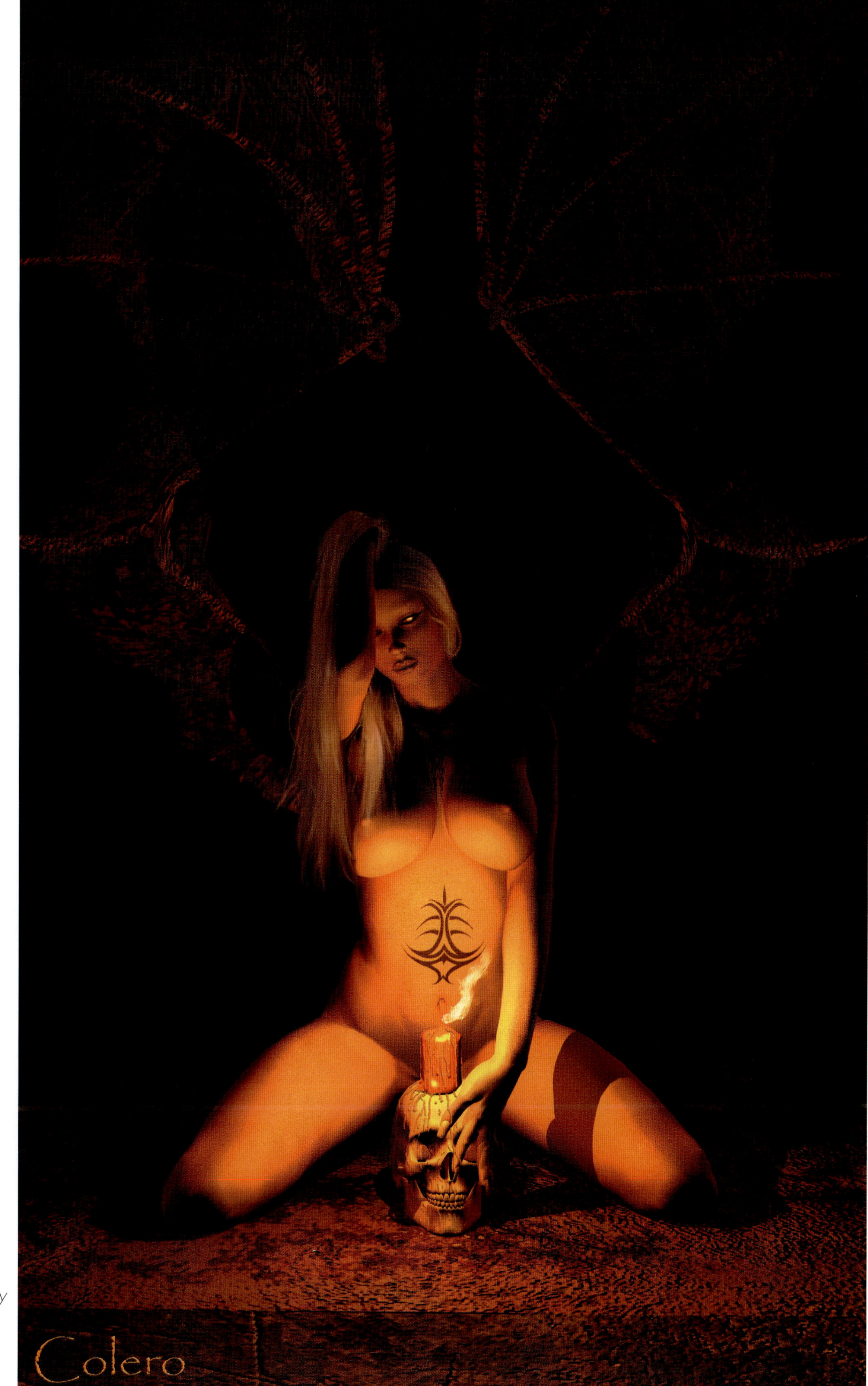

The Seventh Key

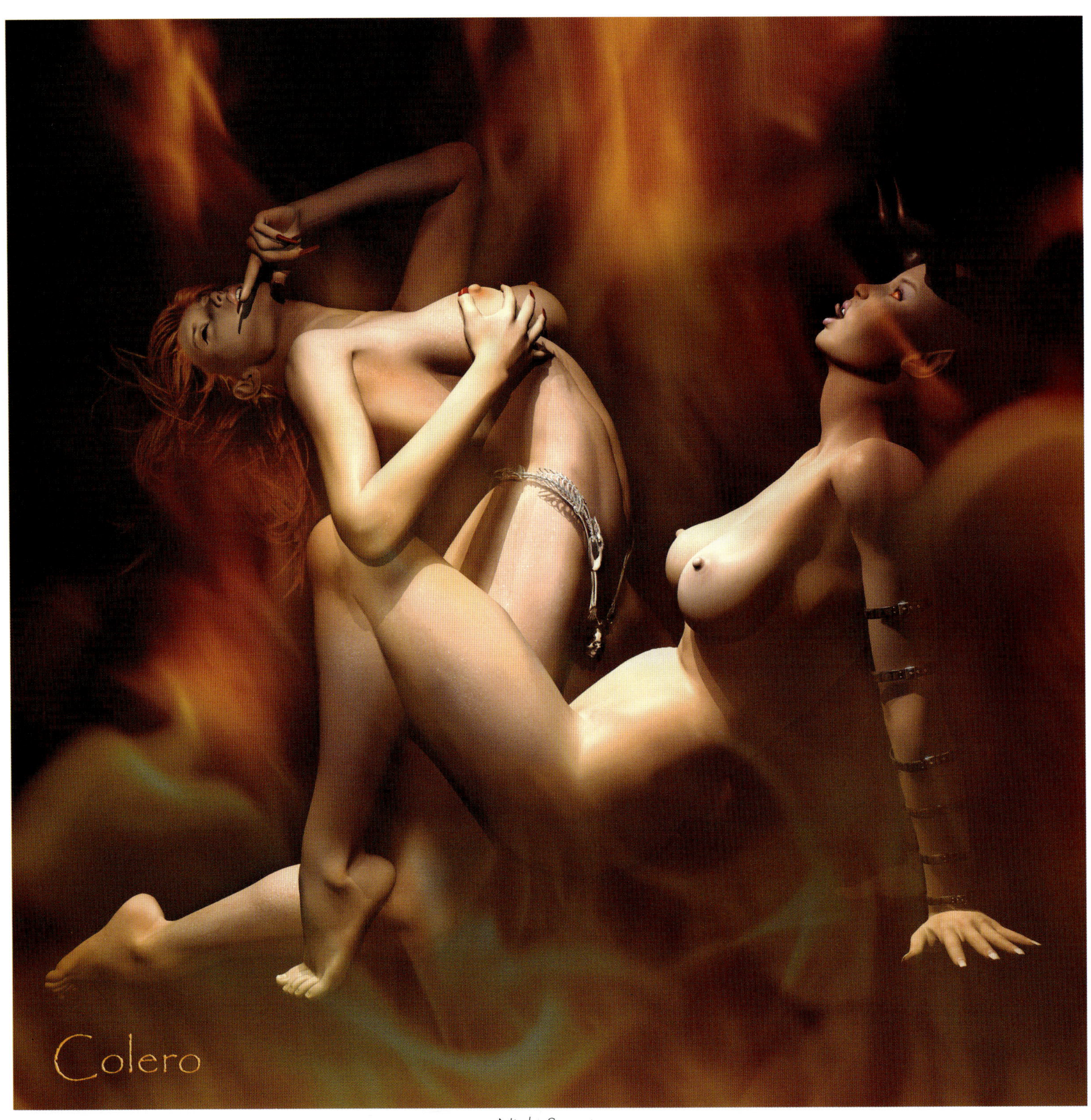

Night Sweats

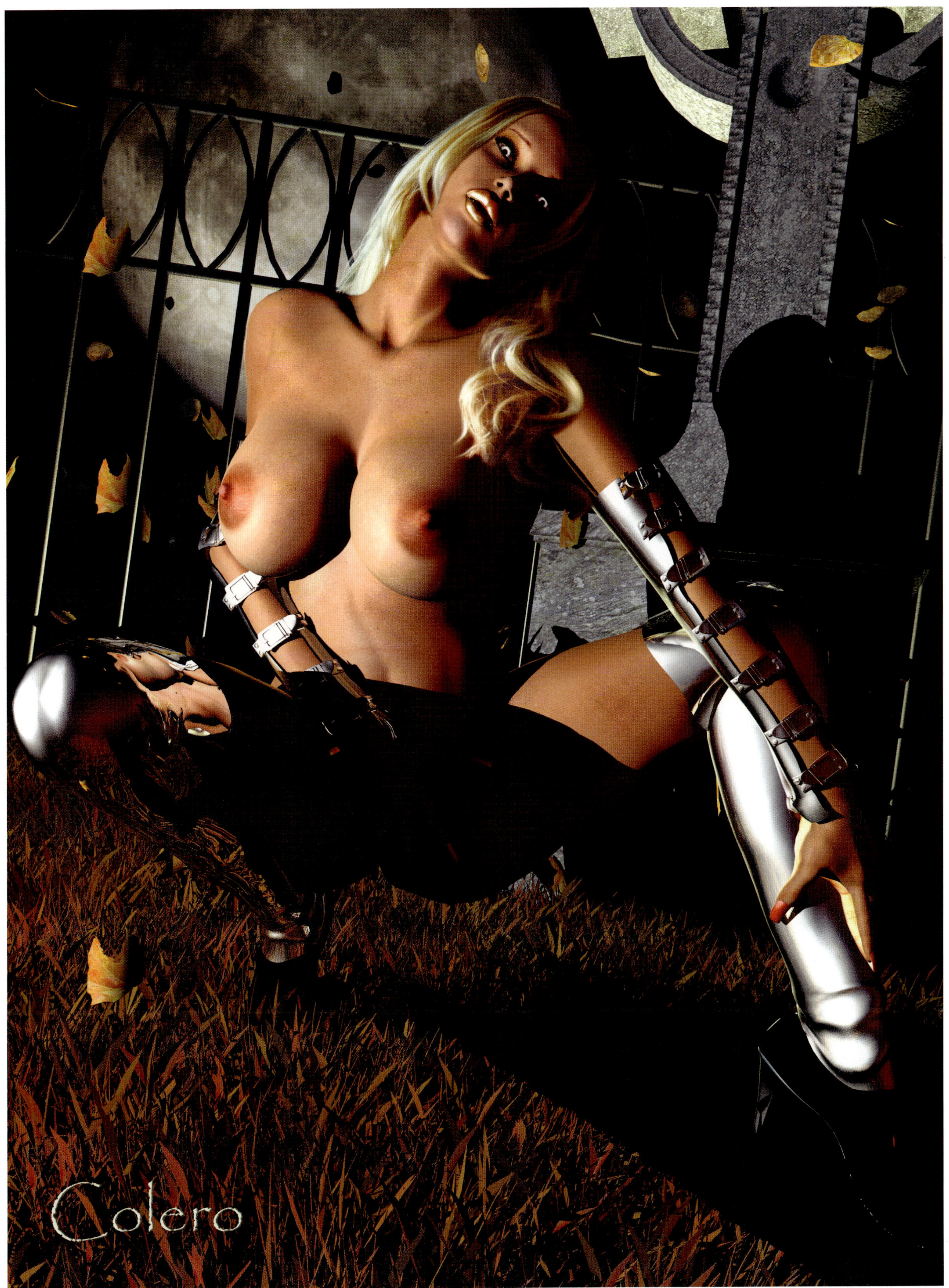

The Damned

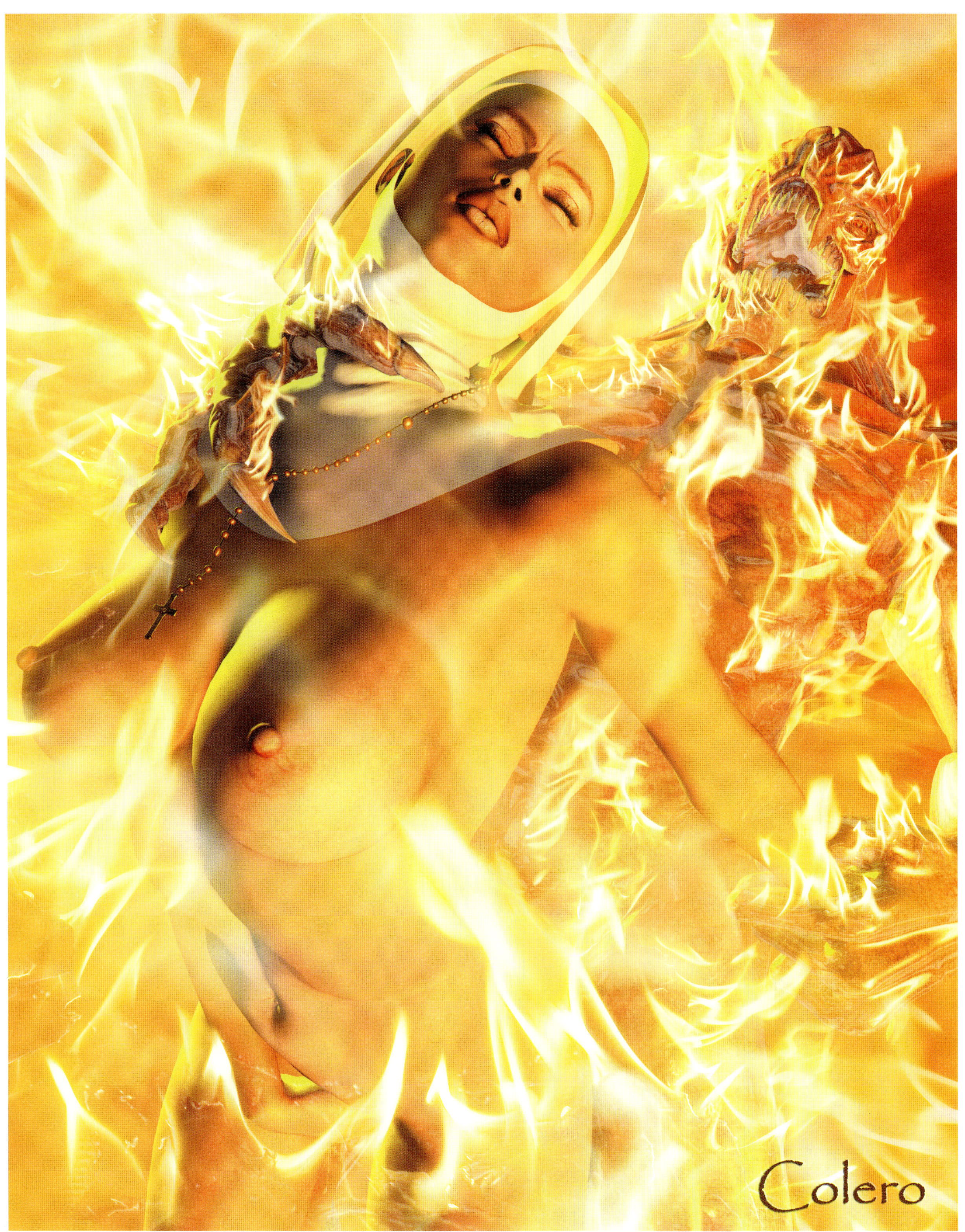

Coitus Cum Demone

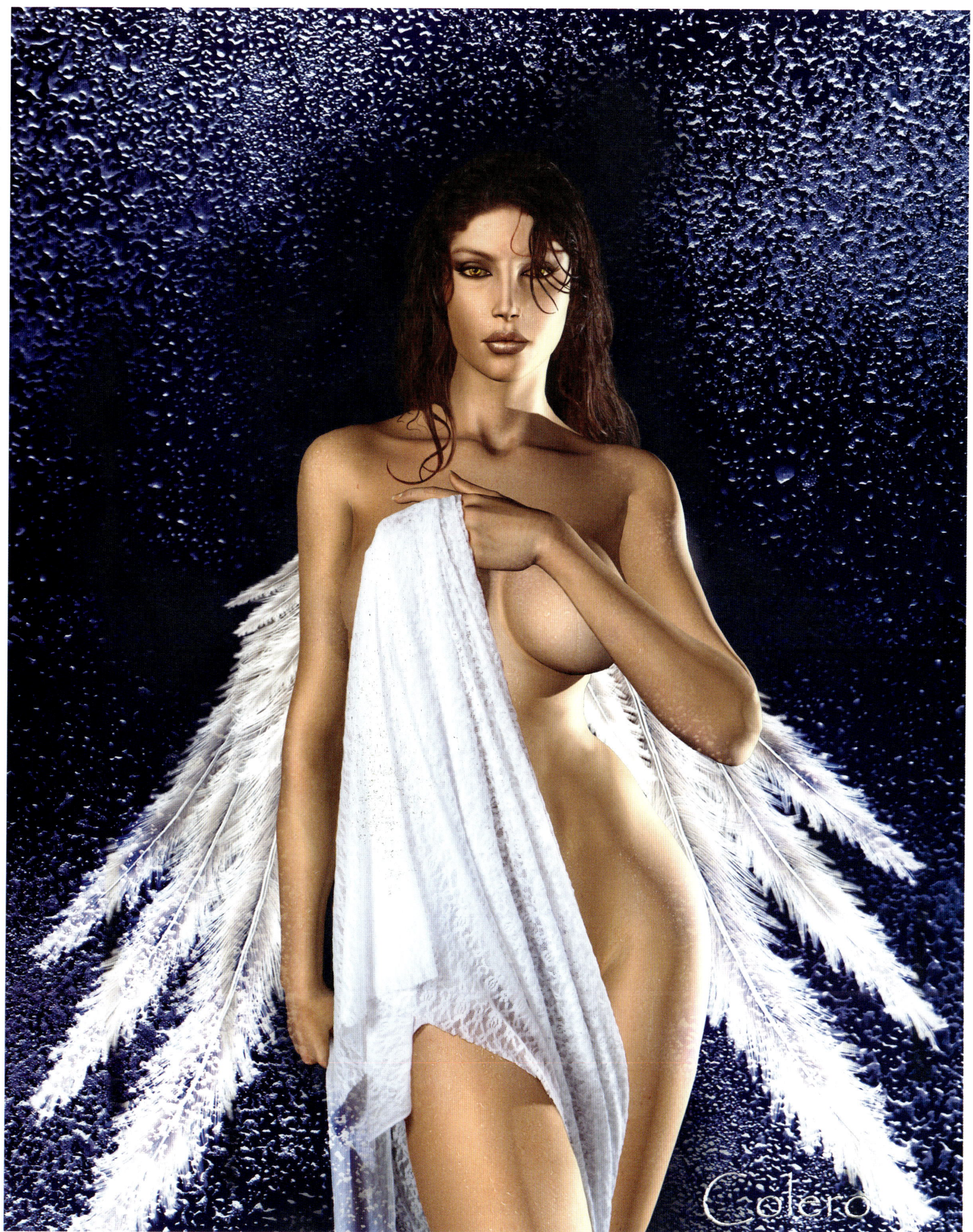

Deliver Me

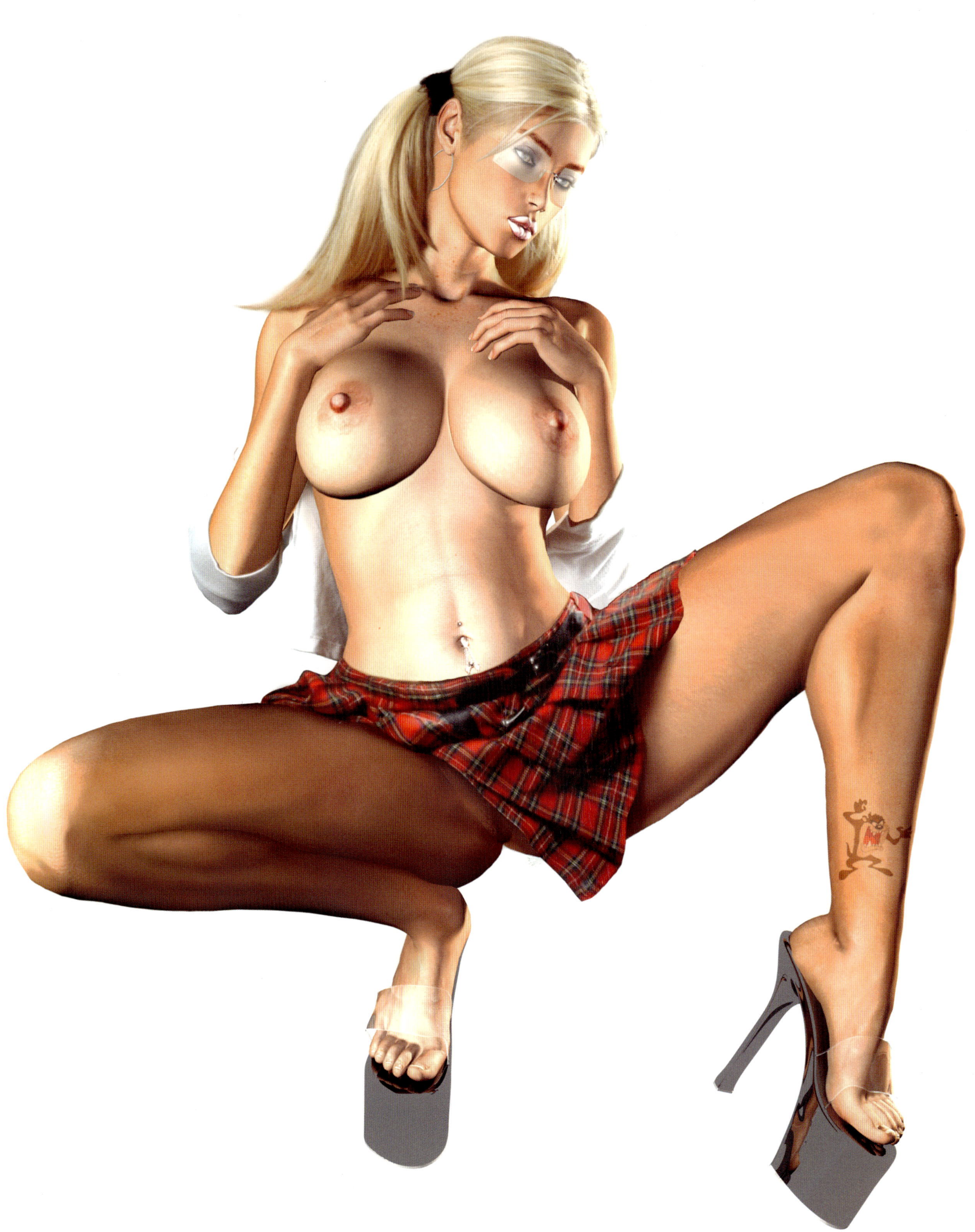

School's In

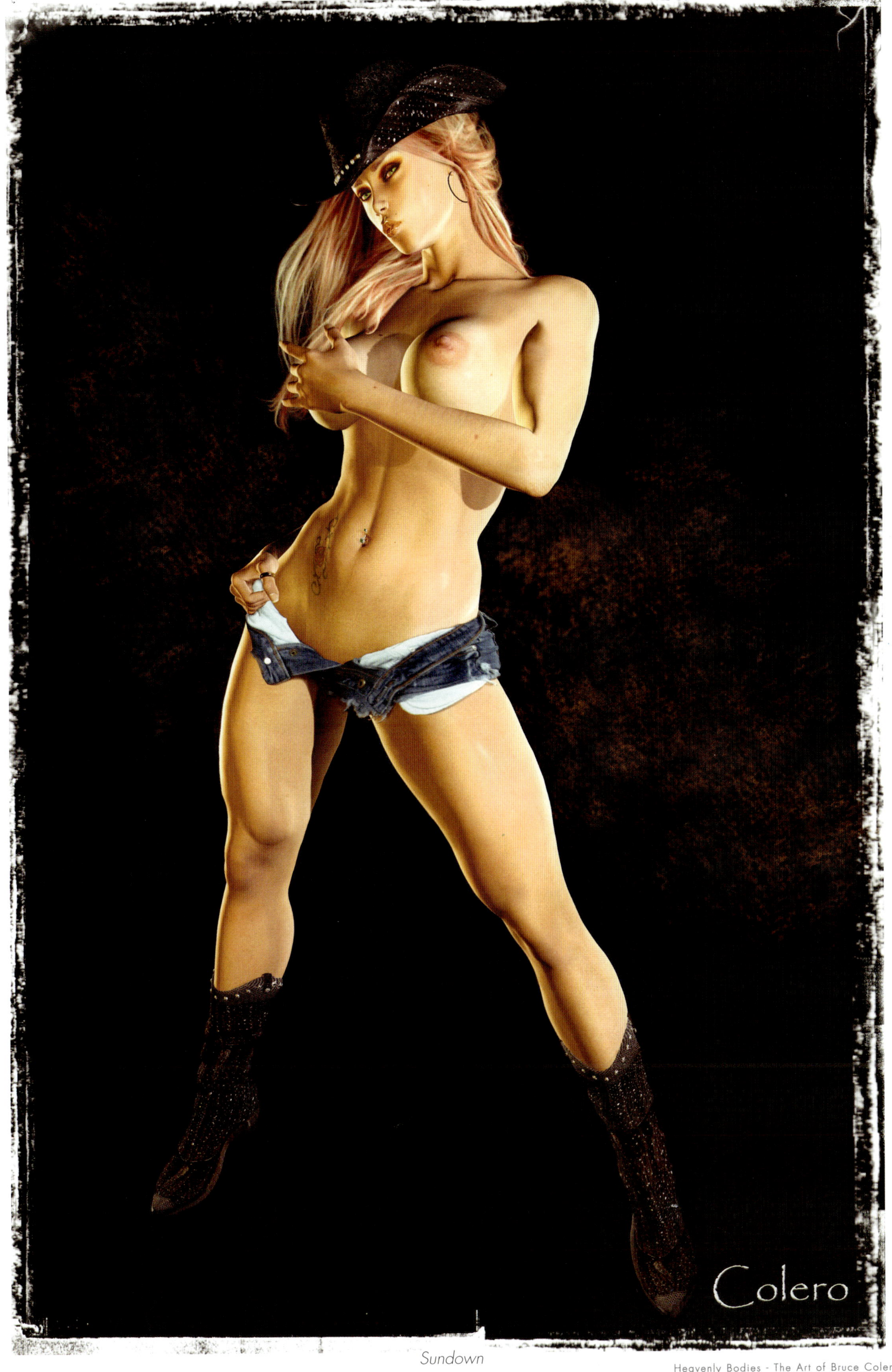

Sundown

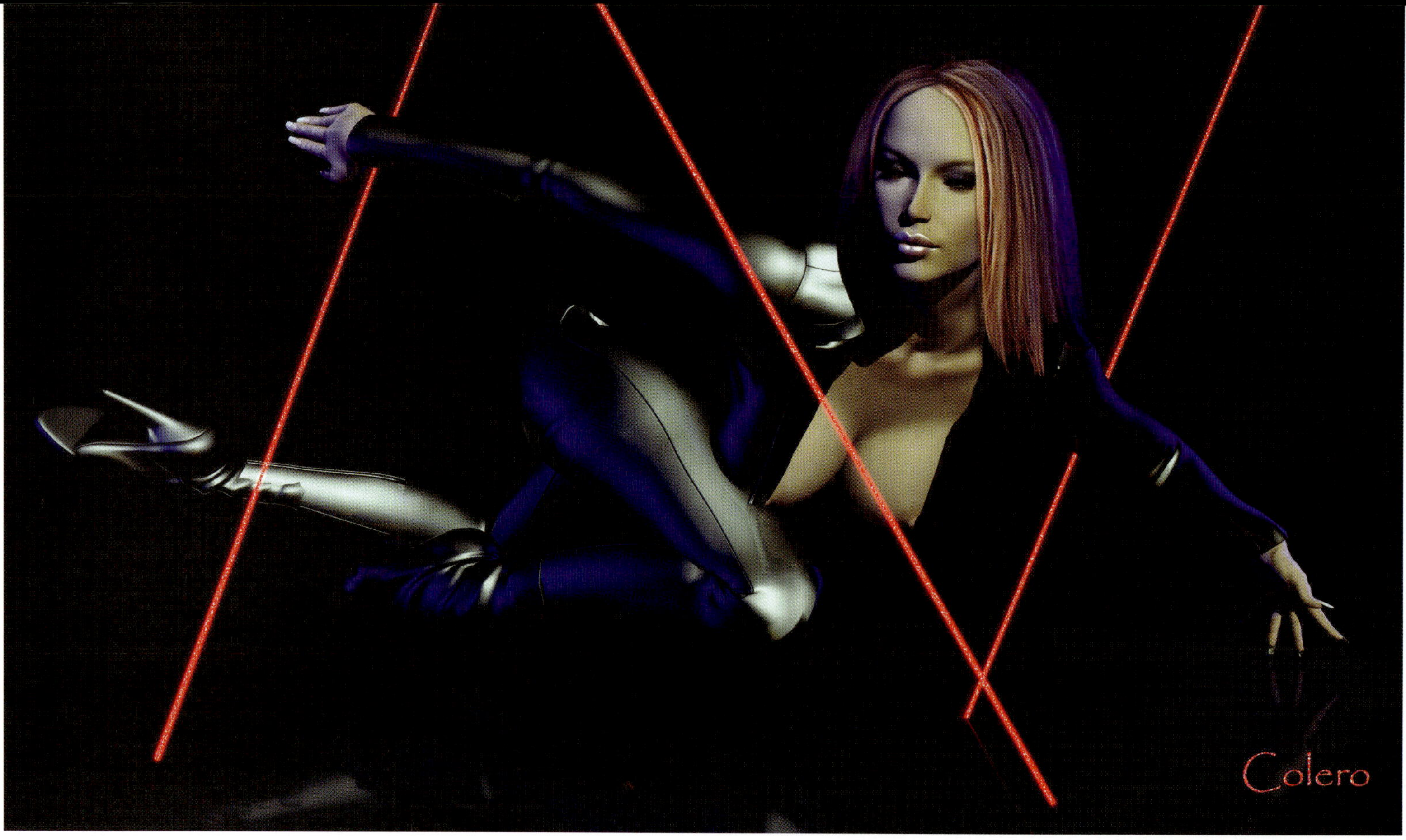

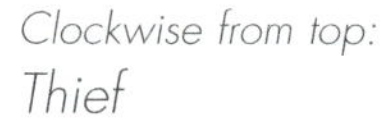

Clockwise from top:
Thief
Bubbles
Idols

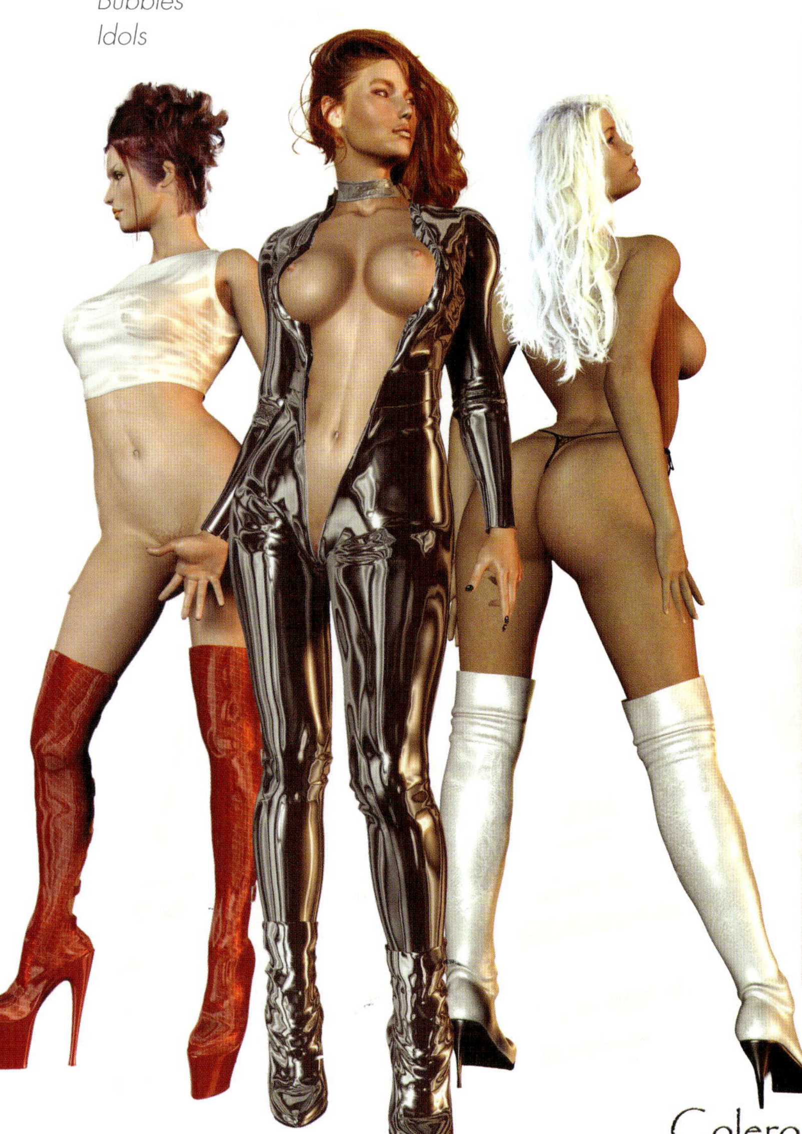

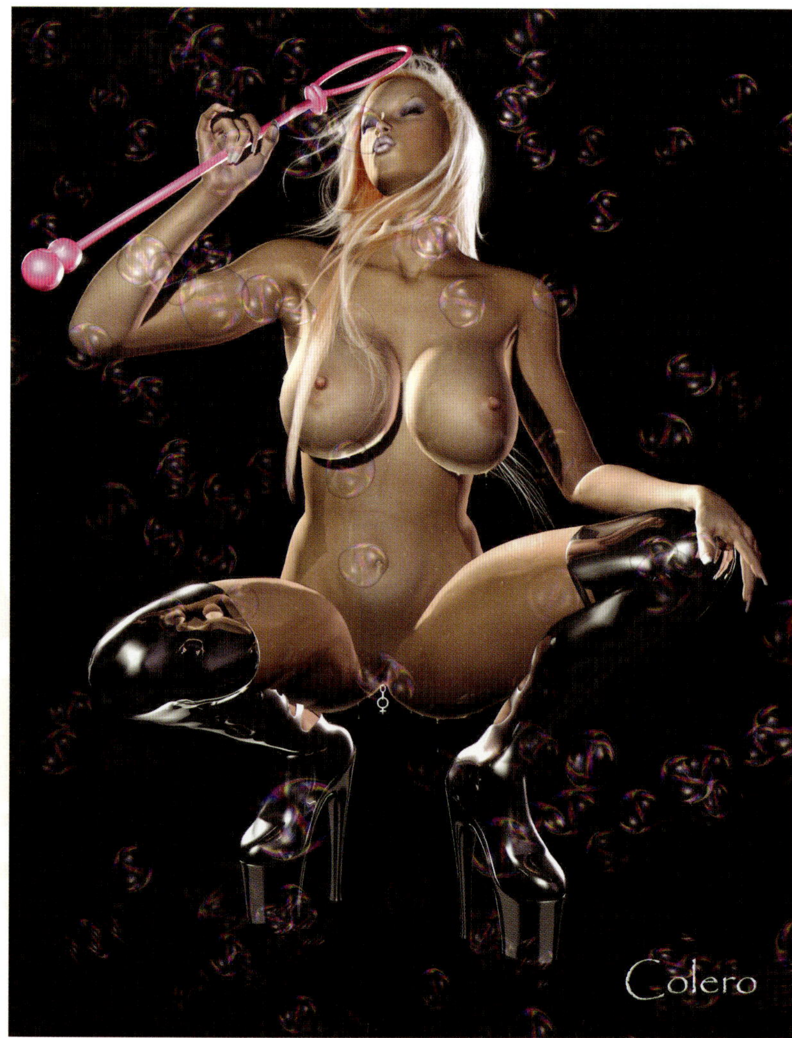

Opposite Page
Maneater

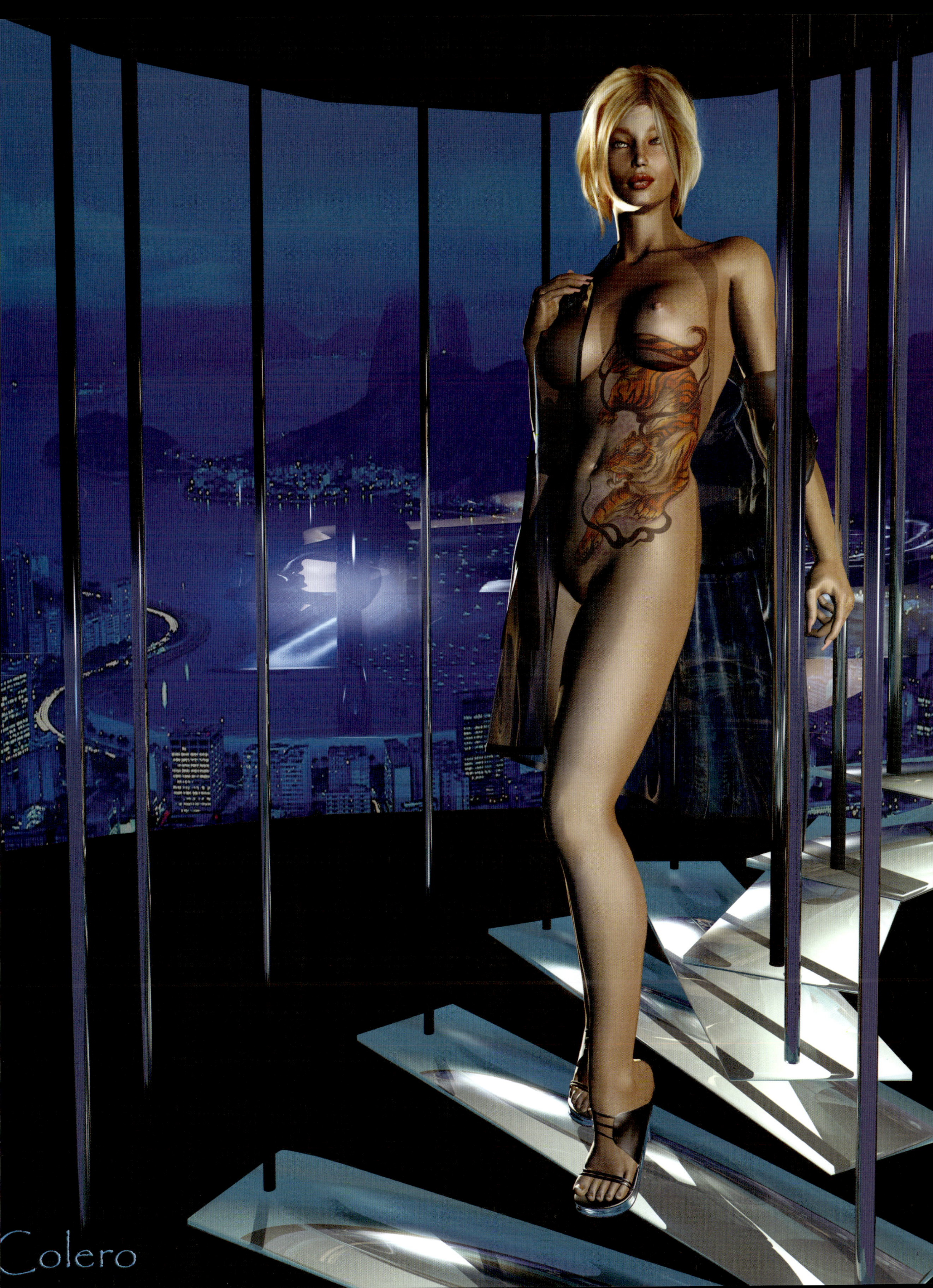
Colero

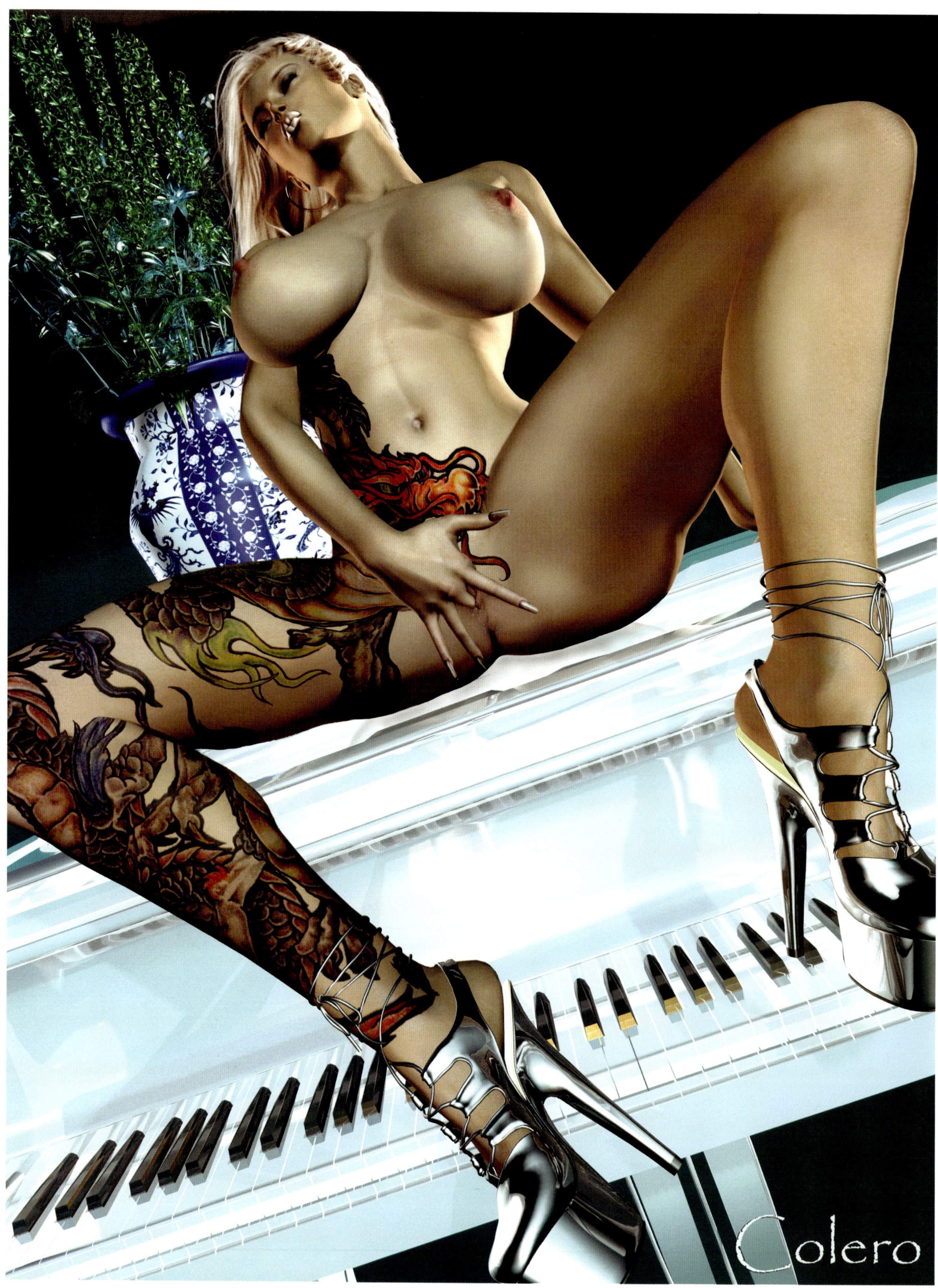

Hum A Few Bars

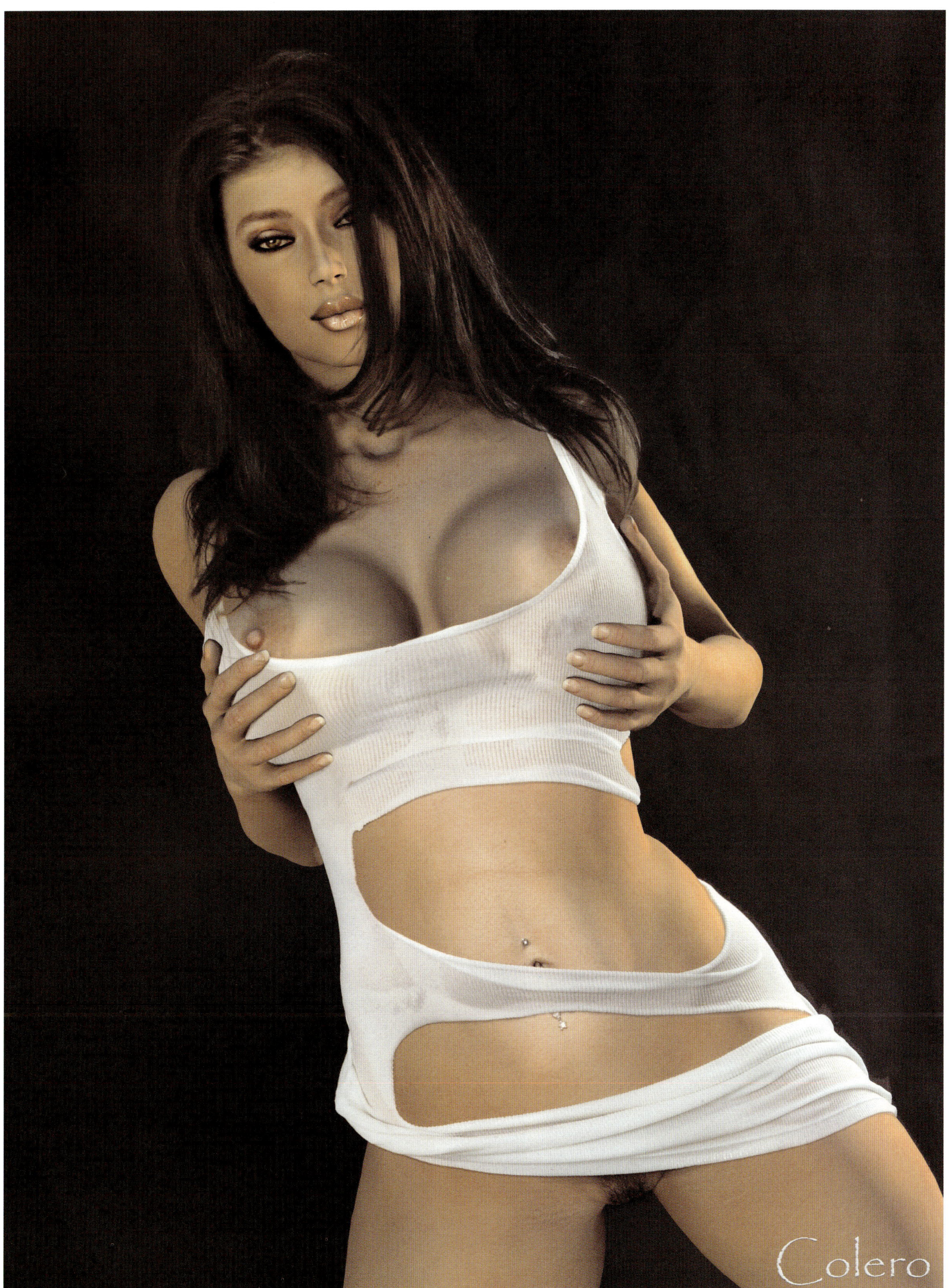

Wifebeater

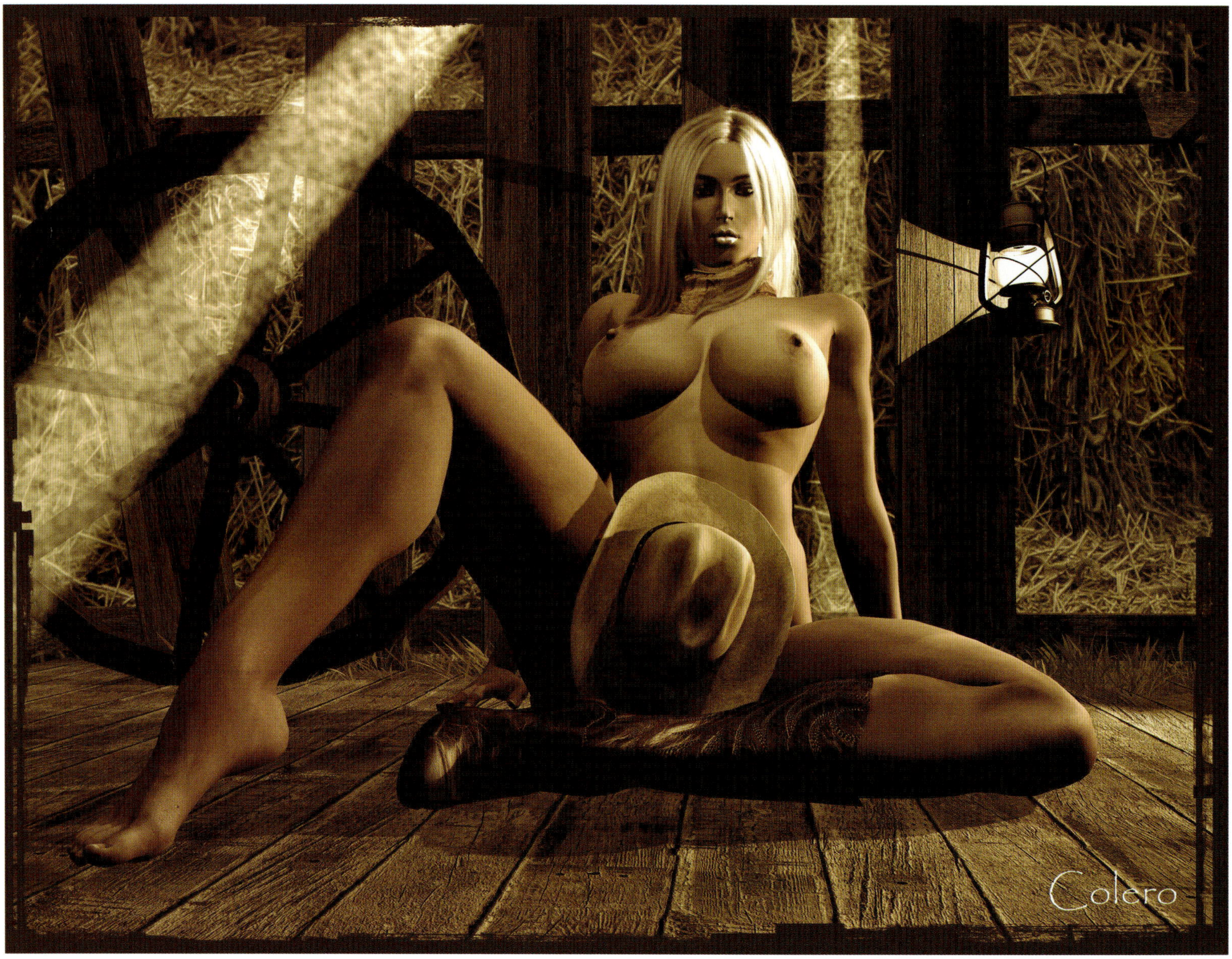

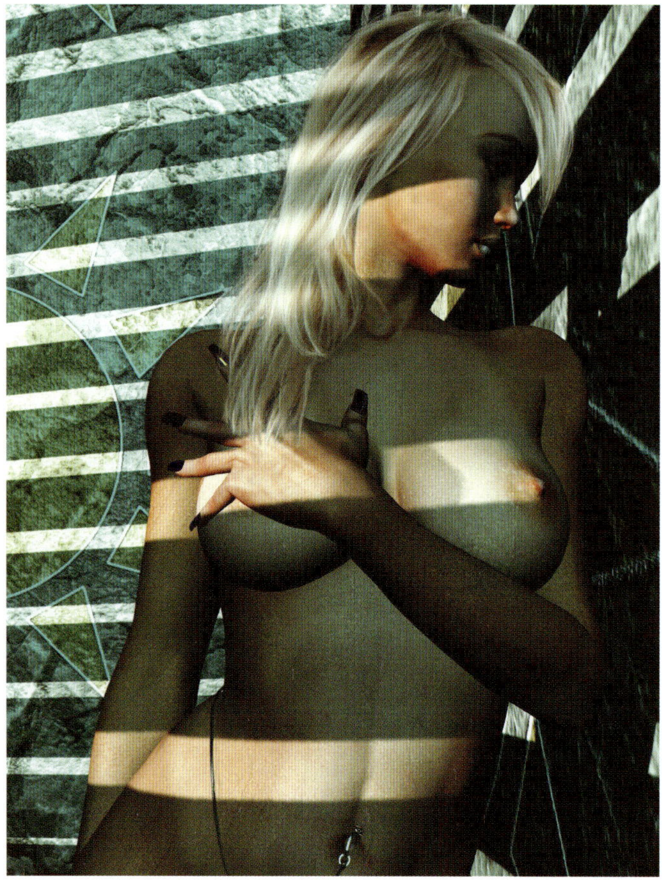

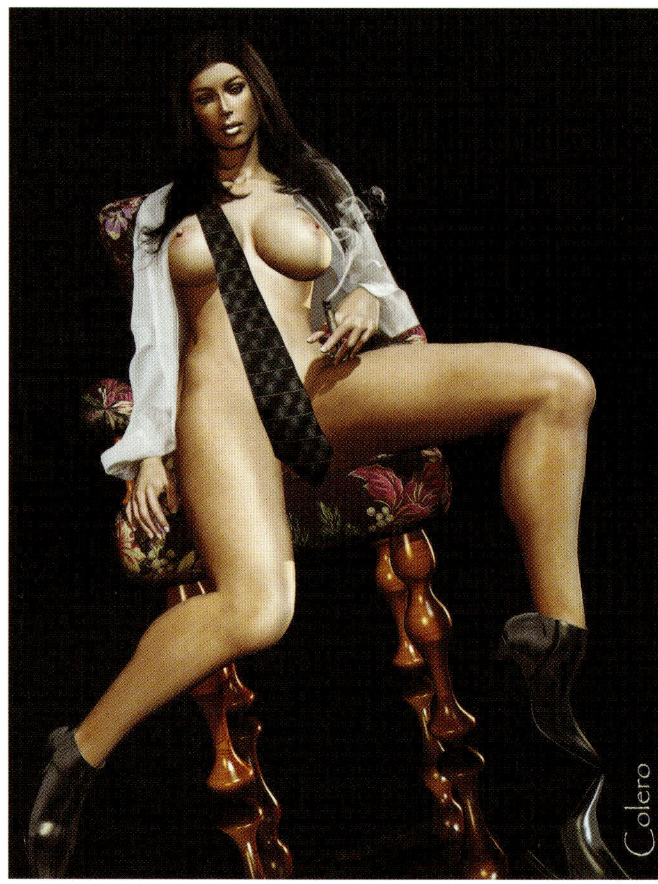

Clockwise from top:
Giddy Up
Smoke
Serenity

Opposite Page:
Hard Target

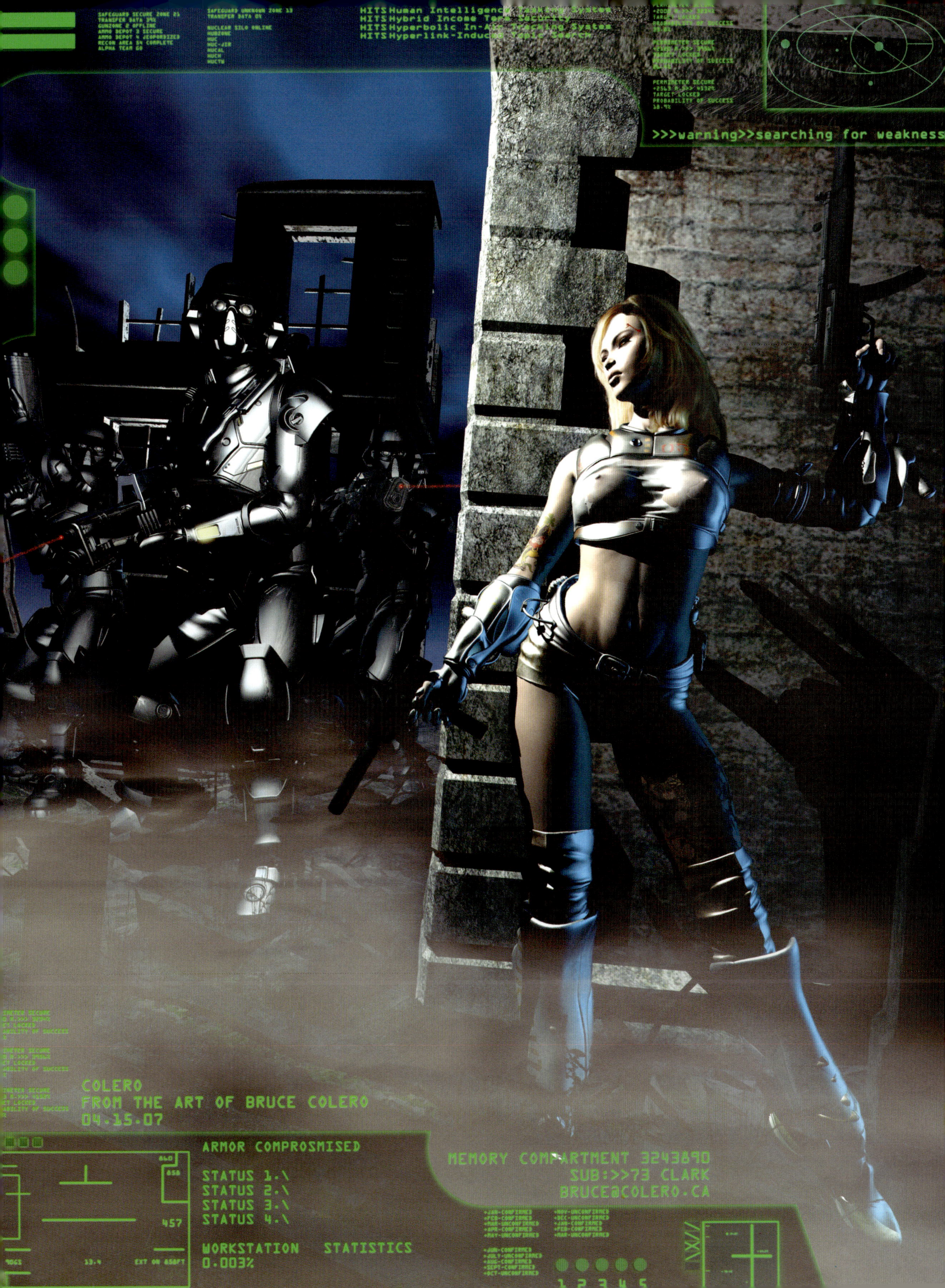

>>>warning>>searching for weakness
COLERO
FROM THE ART OF BRUCE COLERO
04.15.07
ARMOR COMPROSMISED
STATUS 1.\
STATUS 2.\
STATUS 3.\
STATUS 4.\
WORKSTATION STATISTICS
0.003%
MEMORY COMPARTMENT 3243890
SUB:>>73 CLARK
BRUCE@COLERO.CA
1 2 3 4 5

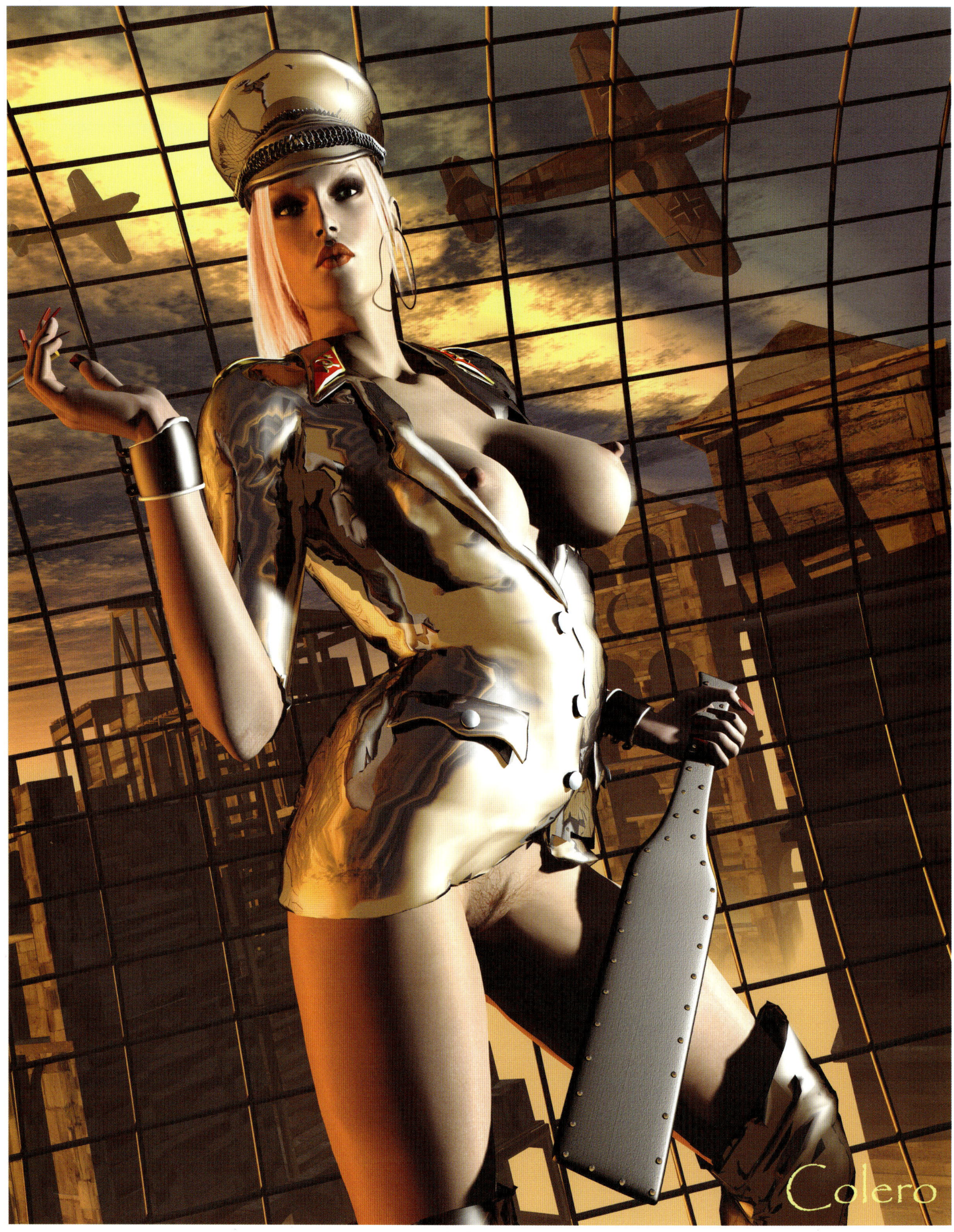

Red Rising

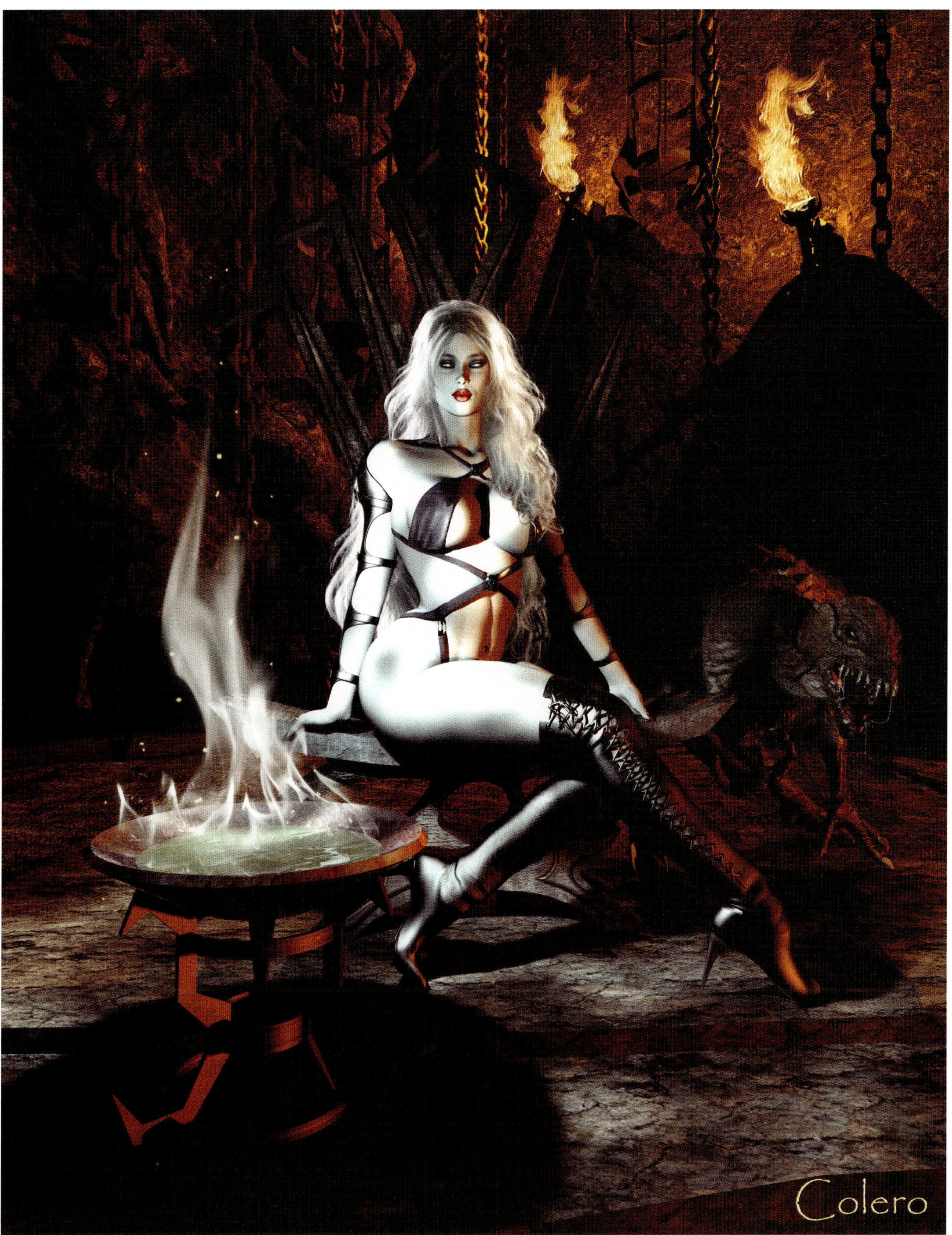

Lady Death

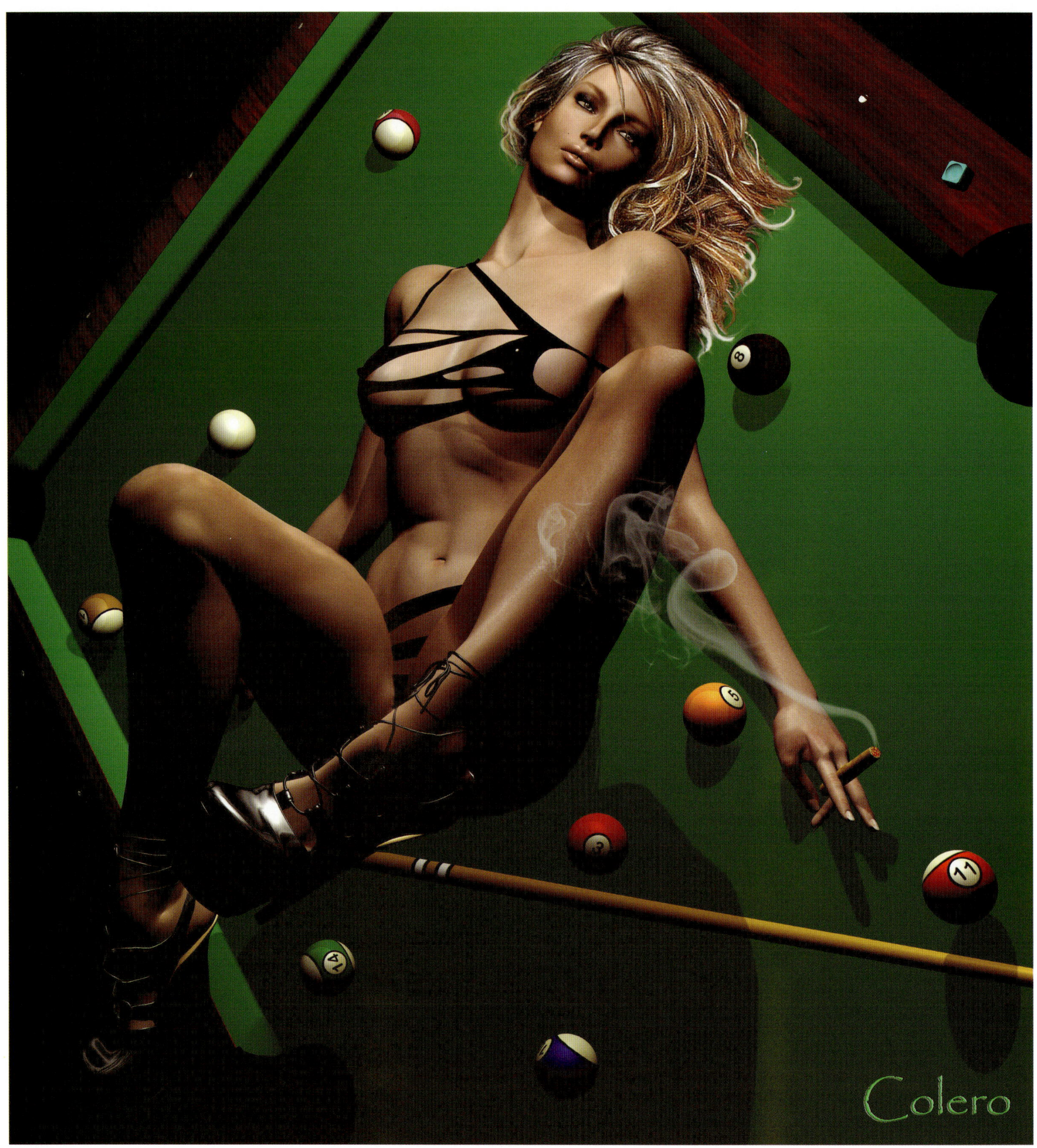

Shark

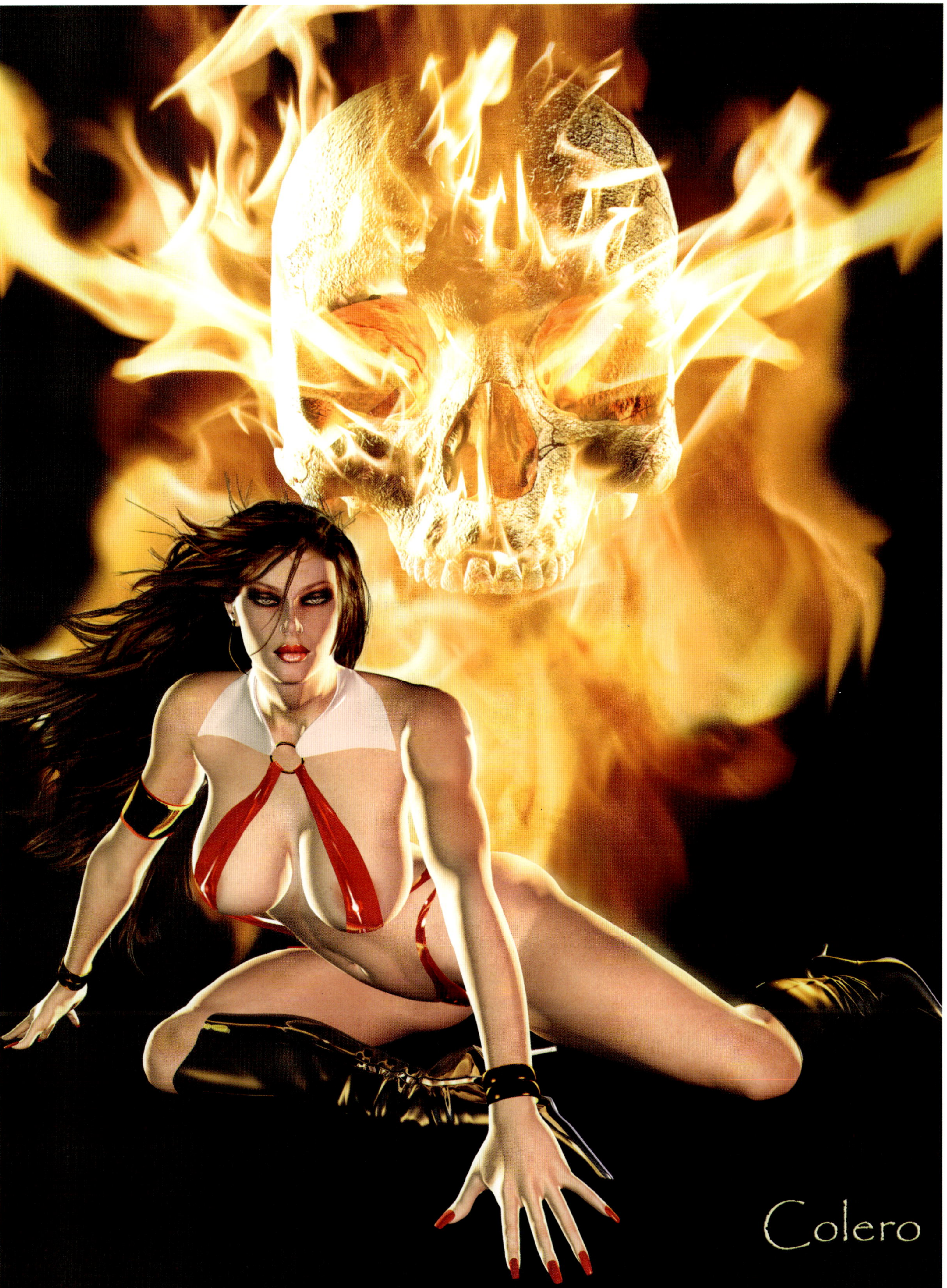

Vampirella

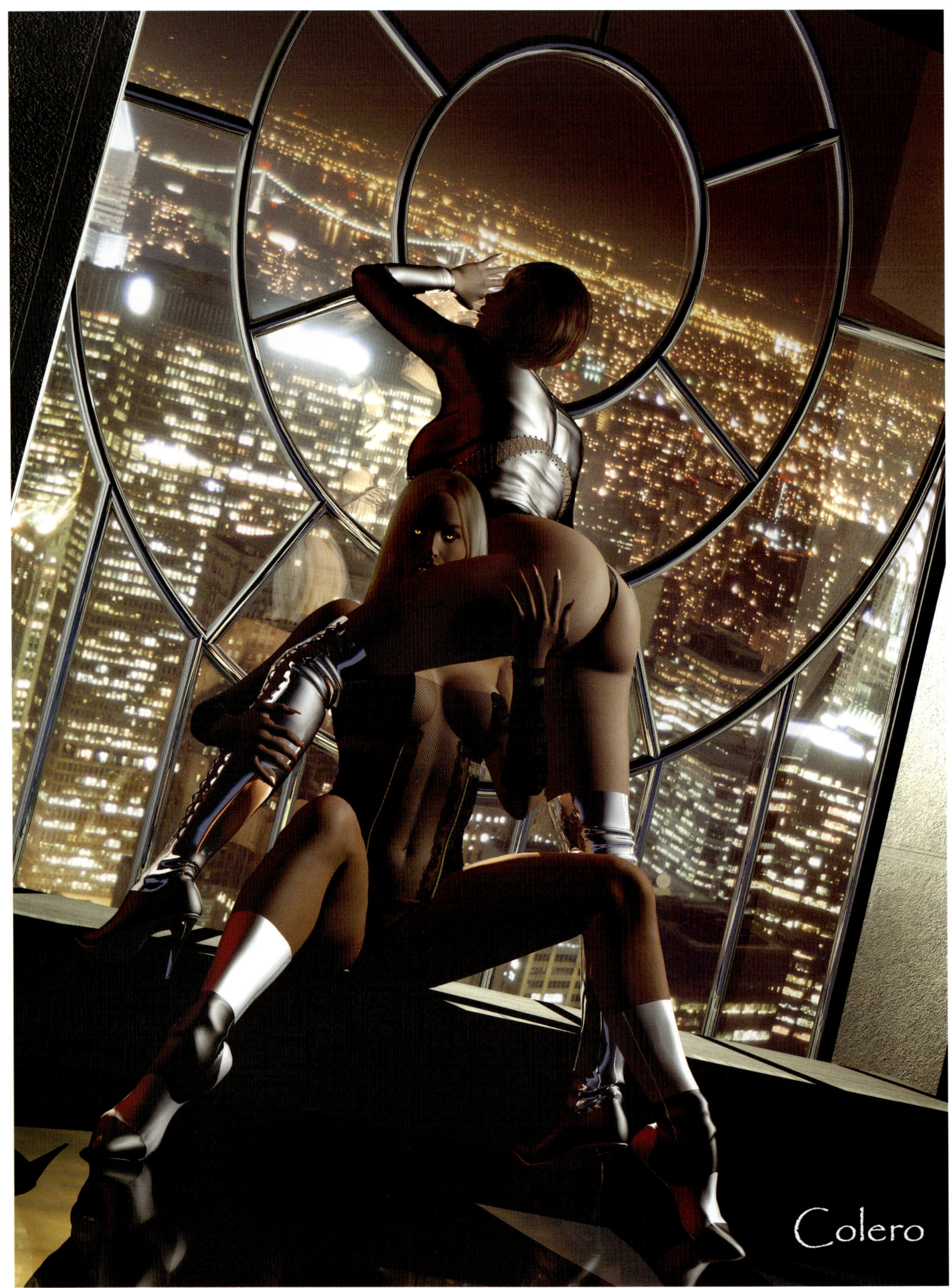

The City Lights

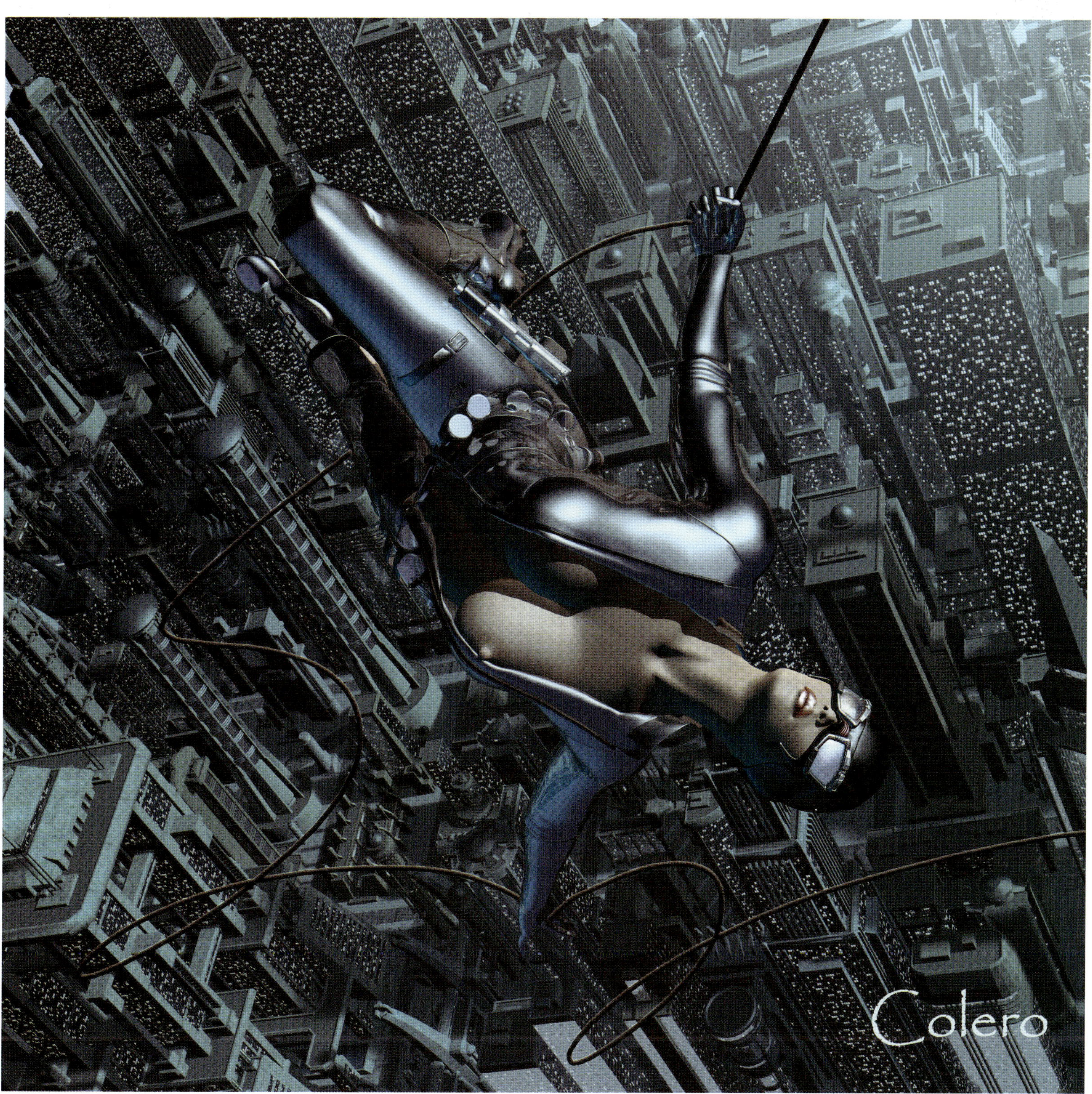

Escape

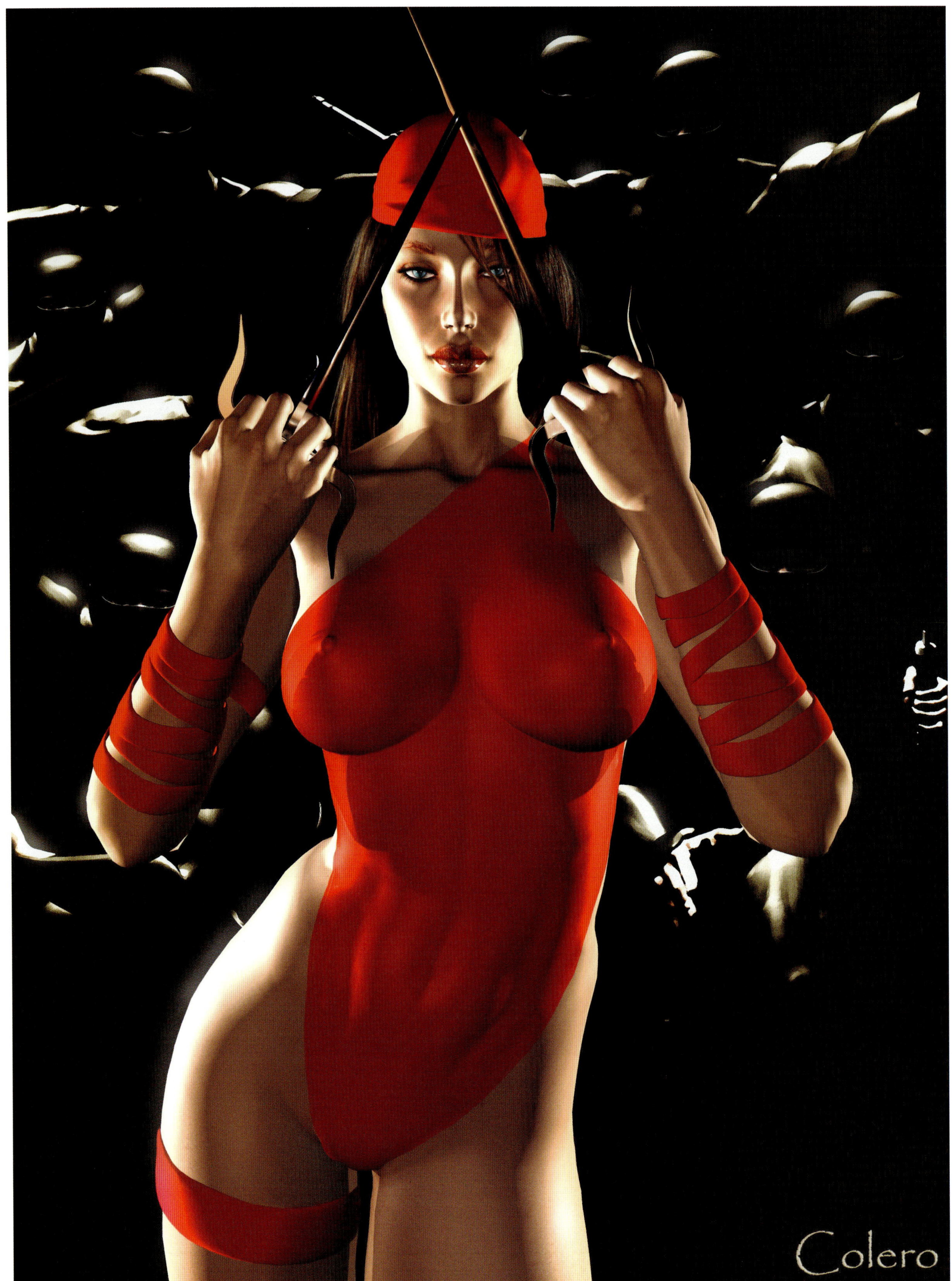

Elektra

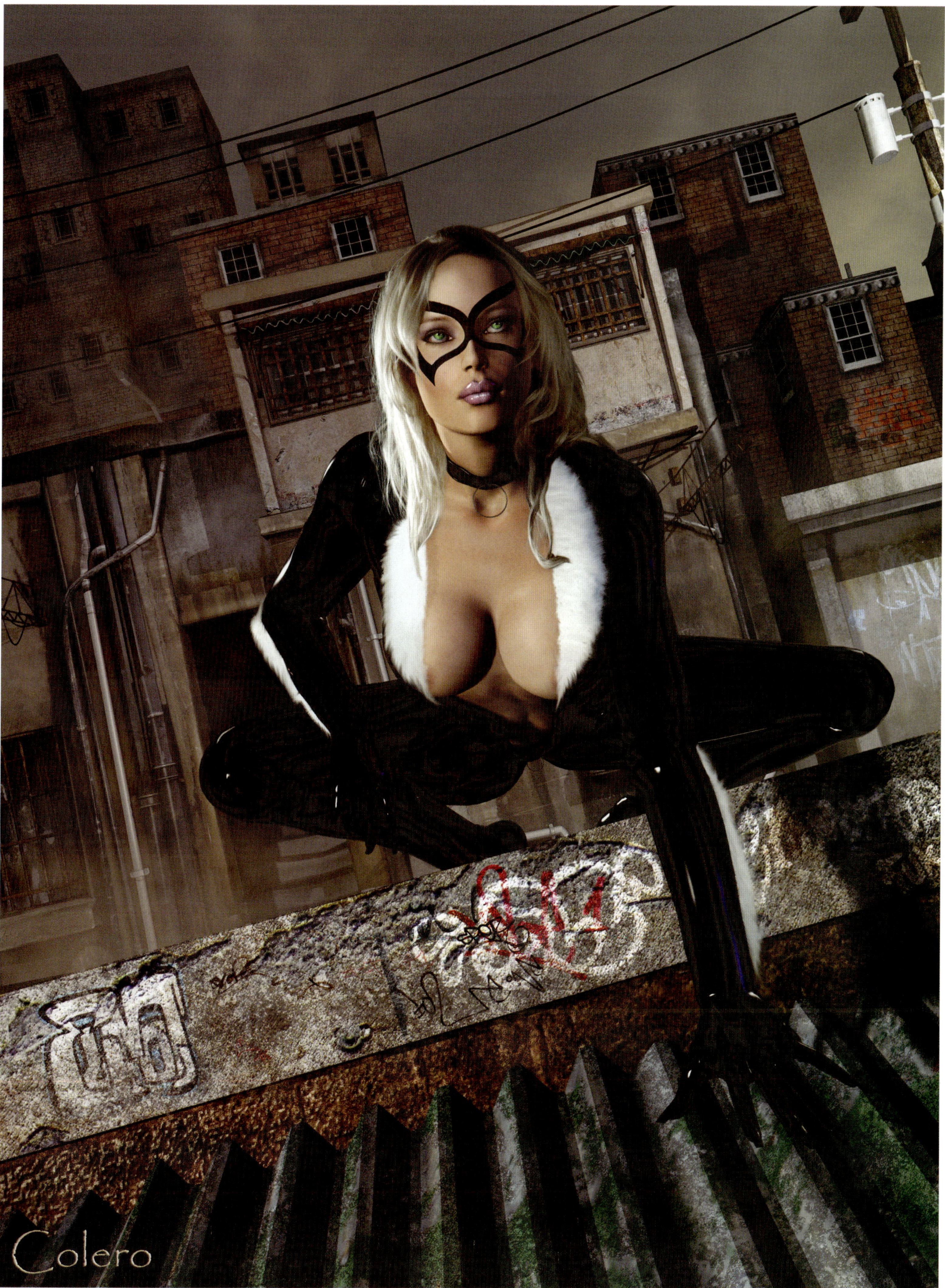

Black Cat

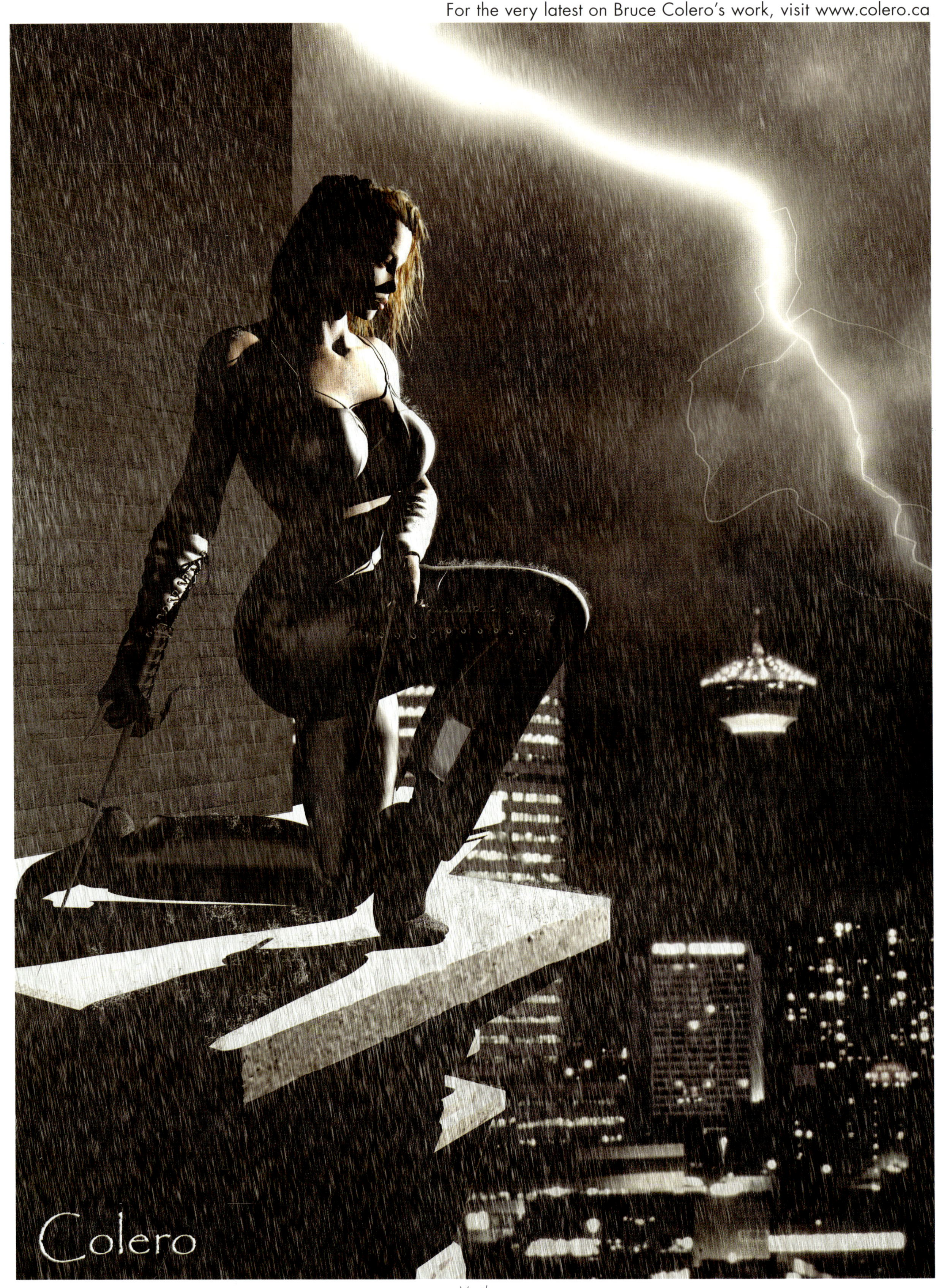

Vigil